CRISIS MANAGEMENT IN CHINESE CONTEXTS

CHINA IN THE 21ST CENTURY

Additional books in this series can be found on Nova's website
under the Series tab.

Additional E-books in this series can be found on Nova's website
under the E-books tab.

PUBLIC HEALTH IN THE 21ST CENTURY

Additional books in this series can be found on Nova's website
under the Series tab.

Additional E-books in this series can be found on Nova's website
under the E-books tab.

CRISIS MANAGEMENT IN CHINESE CONTEXTS

ZENOBIA C. Y. CHAN
EDITOR

Nova Science Publishers, Inc.
New York

NOTICE TO THE READER

The Publisher has taken reasonable care in the preparation of this book, but makes no expressed or implied warranty of any kind and assumes no responsibility for any errors or omissions. No liability is assumed for incidental or consequential damages in connection with or arising out of information contained in this book. The Publisher shall not be liable for any special, consequential, or exemplary damages resulting, in whole or in part, from the readers' use of, or reliance upon, this material. Any parts of this book based on government reports are so indicated and copyright is claimed for those parts to the extent applicable to compilations of such works.

Independent verification should be sought for any data, advice or recommendations contained in this book. In addition, no responsibility is assumed by the publisher for any injury and/or damage to persons or property arising from any methods, products, instructions, ideas or otherwise contained in this publication.

This publication is designed to provide accurate and authoritative information with regard to the subject matter covered herein. It is sold with the clear understanding that the Publisher is not engaged in rendering legal or any other professional services. If legal or any other expert assistance is required, the services of a competent person should be sought. FROM A DECLARATION OF PARTICIPANTS JOINTLY ADOPTED BY A COMMITTEE OF THE AMERICAN BAR ASSOCIATION AND A COMMITTEE OF PUBLISHERS.

Additional color graphics may be available in the E-book version of this book.

LIBRARY OF CONGRESS CATALOGING-IN-PUBLICATION DATA
Crisis management in Chinese contexts / editor, Zenobia C.Y. Chan.
p. ; cm.
Includes bibliographical references and index.
ISBN 978-1-61761-609-9 (hardcover)
1. Disaster medicine--China. 2. Crisis management--China. I. Chan, Zenobia C. Y.
[DNLM: 1. Disaster Planning--China. 2. Risk Management--China. 3. Communicable Disease Control--China. 4. Cultural Characteristics--China. 5. Medical Errors--prevention & control--China. WA 295]
RA645.7.C6C75 2010
362.10951--dc22
2010034027

Published by Nova Science Publishers, Inc. New York

CONTENTS

PREFACE

This book is a collection of various health related issues with the crisis management perspective in Chinese contexts. Crisis management has been well discussed in many disciplines, but in health care settings, little literature has been found to address how crisis management is being conceptualized and implemented with a Chinese cultural sensitivity. So this book serves to address the above inadequacy and offers some lights for what actually healthy related crises in a Chinese society and how health care professions can respond to these crises in a timely and effectively manner with a comprehensively and structurally protocols and plan. The chapter topics include: financial tsunami, human swine influenza, sexually transmitted diseases, medical error, drug recall, adolescent drug abuse, health food crisis and teacher suicide. It is hoped that the diverse topics above can offer some contextual understanding of crises in health realms and how they are responded to within a crisis management framework.

In: Crisis Management in Chinese Contexts   ISBN: 978-1-61761-609-9
Editor: Zenbobia C. Y. Chan   © 2011 Nova Science Publishers, Inc.

Chapter 1

CRISIS MANAGEMENT: A CULTURAL PERSPECTIVE

Wing-Fu Lai[1] and Zenobia C. Y. Chan[2]

[1] University of Hong Kong, Faculty of Science
[2] School of Nursing, The Hong Kong Polytechnic University

SUMMARY

Chinese people, based on the cultural influences, sometimes may tend to be recessive in terms of their crisis management approach. Under such a cultural atmosphere, group members are expected to be loyal to their own organization and always set their organization's interests as the highest priority. In this chapter, we are going to explore the role of Chinese culture in the adoption of crisis management in a Chinese society, and call for proper communication among parties.

OVERVIEW

When a crisis situation happens, covering up crisis usually fails and generally makes a bad situation worse (Yu and Wen, 2003). For this, organizations encountering a crisis are encouraged to tell the truth in a timely

---

[1] Email: rori0610@graduate.hku.hk
[2] Email: hszchan@inet.polyu.edu.hk

manner so that they can meet the expectations of the people involved and the tarnished corporate images can be reestablished (Dougherty, 1992; Barton, 1993; Augustine, 1995; Yu and Wen, 2003). However, in reality, not every organization will tell the truth without hesitation, and not many people would proactively exert pressure on organizations to request them to provide complete and accurate information as fast as possible (Wilcox, Ault and Agee, 1995; Yu and Wen, 2003). As supported by Pepper (1995), who stated, *"Organizations are decision environments and culture plays a primary role in the shaping of the decisions made by organizations and organizational members"* (p. 224), the level of information disclosure in an organization can largely be affected by culture.

CRISIS MANAGEMENT IN CHINESE CULTURE

Chinese culture is largely shaped by Confucianism (Chen & Chung, 1994; Yu and Wen, 2003), whose present-oriented and pragmatic philosophical notion strongly impacts practices in China (Yum, 1997, p. 76). Confucianism considers proper human relationships as the basis of a society (Yum, 1997), and, in total, has four core principles that guide a man's proper conduct (Yum, 1997).

The first core principle is "humanism", the warm, human feelings shared among people (Yu and Wen, 2003). Confucius advocated that when one dislikes something in the person to your right, it is improper to pass it on to the person on one's left (Yum, 1997). The second core principle in Confucianism is "faithfulness,"which is the level of loyalty in a relationship and determines the righteousness of human deeds in terms of the societal good rather than personal notions of profit (Yu and Wen, 2003). By emphasizing proper social relationships and their maintenance, rather than any abstract concern for a general collective body, faithfulness and humanism extend Hofstede's (1980) notion of collectivism (Yum, 1997; Yu and Wen, 2003). This value system runs deep in China and extends to its organizational culture. Both "humanism" and "faithfulness" are the grounding common values of Chinese culture, and most of the organizational and interpersonal contexts of daily interactions in China are guided by these traditional notions (Yu and Wen, 2003).

Furthermore, Chinese people, based on the cultural influences, may at times tend to be recessive in terms of their crisis management approach. This can refer to ideas suggested by the Confucian. In the book *Analectic*, the idea, "Understand the order of Heaven (Zhi Tian Ming)," is mentioned.

"Understand[ing] the decrees of Heaven" does not mean that people should totally rely on god or supernatural beings. In fact, it emphasizes that there is objective constraint out there. Once you try your best to do something, then it will be all right. There is always something that we cannot control (Confucius,1958). Confucian reminds people that they should always maintain this kind of mindset no matter what they do they do and face, including when they encounter crisis.

Barring the aforementioned, saving face is another factor governing attitudes adopted by Chinese people in crisis management (Yu and Wen, 2003). As mentioned above, family is the basic and most characteristic unit of all social institutions in China, and, in the Confucian sense, family affection is believed to play the role of binding together all relations in a society (Chai & Chai, 1965). The family metaphor can be translated to all manner of group and organizational relations in a community (Yu and Wen, 2003). Under such a cultural atmosphere, group members are expected to be loyal to their own organization and always set their organization's interests as the highest priority. They need to prevent losing the face of their group as much as they can. The discourse "face" here, as suggested by Goffman (1959, 1971), is one's socially approved self-image. Over the years, "saving face" appears to be a traditional value frequently mentioned in most literature (e.g. Pye, 1988). Under the notion of saving face, as depicted by a well-known Chinese saying, "Ugly things in our family shall not go public," silence has become a virtue in Chinese culture, and is much preferred to being frank or forthright and make waves (Yu and Wen, 2003).

Apart from the tendency to keep the "ugly things" silent, people understand that there is always something out of their control. They have faith in animism, and this also largely shapes their ideology towards crisis. Chinese people respect nature very much and strongly believe in it (Gu 2005). They would believe in supernatural power when they come across any crises, and offer sacrifices to their ancestors. Also, they are superstitious about ghosts or spirits (Fung & Shi 2001). So, people would ask the supernatural beings for advice, which is known as divination, when they face difficulties. For example, the emperor would offer sacrifices to gods and ancestors every year. The aim was to maintain the well-being of the state. In times facing crises, such as drought or epidemic, offering sacrifices to the supernatural beings was common in order to stay out of these troubles and difficulties (Fung & Shi 2001). During the late Qing dynasty, the Boxers, who appealed to the public by using supernatural powers, successfully got the support of the public when the Qing government was too weak to resist the foreign intervention (Liu

2010). This historical fact shows that Chinese people usually rely on some supernatural power to solve their difficulty, even when they encounter national crisis.

CALL FOR COMMUNICATION

In fact, based on the nature of crises, crisis management could be of multiple contexts. In the health contexts, as long as health risks associated with disasters are involved, the role of public health within a community and for homeland security is imperative (Gomez, Passerini, and Hare, 2006; Hooke and Rogers; 2005). In order to ensure proper crisis management, accurate information must be communicated to the public on a timely basis, and public attitudes or behaviors have to be manipulated in an interactive way (Gomez, Passerini, and Hare, 2006; Rice & Katz, 2001). Unfortunately, proper crisis communication and information disclosure is not easy in China. Chinese people will usually attempt to cover a shameful truth.

As suggested by Historian Bo (1985) in *The Ugly Chinese*, Chinese people seldom confess their faults. They will do everything to cover their mistakes (Bo, 1985). In reality, this can potentially hamper communication in management practices when crises come. This could be exemplified by the melamine contamination event in China in 2008, during which the relevant parties attempted to "cover up" or "ignore" the abnormally high prevalence of renal stone cases discovered since July 2008, and which finally resulted in global public health problems (Chan and Lai, 2009).

In fact, communication and proper information disclosure are essential to crisis management. As suggested by Marra (1998), the major factors influencing the success of crisis management are the underlying communication culture and the extent of autonomy of the parties involved. Unfortunately, there is a serious paucity of literature discussing cultural influences on this aspect (Marra, 1998). Actually, exploration of communication enhancement and the cultural implications are especially important in the Chinese context as Chinese people are socialized to remain silent when they are facing highly uncertain situations (Yu and Wen, 2003).

Many Chinese sayings illustrate the value of silence in Chinese society, for example, "*Trouble is born out of the words you speak*" (Yu and Wen, 2003). Because of the Confucian philosophy and some historical reasons, unnecessary communications are deemed to risk oneself unnecessarily. Further, in order to save face, Chinese people seldom talk about their problems. In this, they are taught to always keep "silent" and attempt to cover things up. This could be illustrated by Oliver (1971), who mentioned that Chinese people regard speaking about sensitive subject matter as an unwise commitment of judgment (Oliver, 1971). In fact, a clearly mapped, enabled and coordinated communication pattern across multiple boundaries must be well-established to manage crisis (Gomez, Passerini, and Hare, 2006). The implications of organizational emergencies, such as Tylenol, Three Mile Island, Bhopal, and Exxon Valdez (Turoff, *et al.*, 2004), can have a macro-social effect causing harm to people outside of the organizational control or periphery (Gomez, Passerini, and Hare, 2006). For this, when a crisis comes, collaboration between different parties should be made to combat the situation.

CONCLUDING REMARKS

According to *The Oxford English Dictionary* (1989), crisis can be understood as times of difficulty, insecurity, and suspense, especially in politics or commerce aspects. Crisis management is an approach to handling emergencies, in which preparation, timing, communication and coordination are a *sine qua non*. However, its practice varies among different cultures and beliefs. As informed by past experiences during health emergencies, parties always have to resolve the crisis tasks with limited information (Gomez, Passerini, and Hare, 2006). For this, in order to cope with the situation, cross-disciplinary collaboration, technological coordination and communication are imperative (Tan and Benbasat, 1993; Lim and Benbasat, 2000; Goodhue and Thompson, 1995; Vessey, 1991; Vessey and Galetta, 1991).

ACKNOWLEDGMENTS

The authors would like to thank Shelley Man-Hoi Tsang (an independent scholar) and Dorothy Kwok (School of Nursing, Hong Kong Polytechnic University) for their help during the writing help of this chapter.

AUTHOR'S BACKGROUND

Wing-Fu Lai graduated from the University of Hong Kong with a bachelor's degree in food and nutritional science. He was on the Dean's Honors List 2005/06 and 2006/07 of the Faculty of Science, and is currently pursuing a Ph.D. degree in chemical biology. He can be contacted at rori0610@graduate.hku.hk.

REFERENCES

Augustine, N. R. (1995, November-December). Managing the crisis you tried to prevent. *Harvard Business Review*, 147-158.

Barton, L. (1993). *Crisis in organizations: Managing and communicating in the heat of chaos*. Cincinnati, OH: South-Western.

Bo, Y. (1985). *The ugly Chinese.* Taipei: Shin Kwang.

Chai, C, & Chai, W. (1965). *The Scared Books of Confucius and Other Confucian Classics.* New Hyde Park, NY: University Books.

Chan, Z. C. Y., and Lai, W. F. (2009). Revisiting the melamine contamination event in China: Implications for ethics in food technology, *Trends in Food Science and Technology*, 20(8): 366-373.

Chen, G., and Chung, J. (1994). The impact of Confucianism on organizational communication. *Communication Quarterly, 42,* 93-10

Confucius (1958). *Lun Yu Yi Zhu.* Beijing : Zhonghua.

Dougherty, D. (1992). *Crisis Communications: What Every Executive Needs to Know*. New York: Walker and Company.

Feng, L. Y. and Shi, W. M. (2001). *Zhong Guo Wen Hua Lë Ying.* Beijing: Wu Zhou Chuan Bo Chu Ban She.

Goffman, E, (1959). *The Presentation of Self in Everyday Life.* New York: Anchor Books.

Goffman, D. (1971). *Relations in Public.* New York: Basic Books.

Gomez, EA, Passerini, K., and Hare, K. (2006). Public health crisis management: community level roles and communication options, *Proceedings of the 3rd Annual ISCRAM*, Newark, NJ.

Goodhue, D.L., and Thompson, R.L. (1995). Task-technology fit and individual performance. *MIS Quarterly*, 19, 213-236.

Gu, W. L. (2005). *Zhong Guo Wen Hua Tong Lun.* Shanghai Shi: Hua Dong Shi Fan Da Xue Chu Ban She

Hofsede, G. (1980). *Culture's Consequences.* Newbury, CA: Sage

Hooke, W. and Rogers, P. (2005). *Public Health Risks of Disasters: Communication, Infrastructure, and Preparedness Workshop Summary.* Washington DC: The National Academics Press.

Lim, K.H. and Benbasat, I. (2000). The effect of multimedia on perceived equivocality and perceived usefulness of information systems. *MIS Quarterly*, 24(3), 449-471.

Liu, H. (2010) An analysis of the intentions of the superstitious practices by Boxers. *Journal of Heibei Normal University(Philosophy)*, 33(1), 112-116.

Marra, F. J. (1998). Crisis communication plans: Poor predictors of excellent crisis public relations. *Public Relations Review, 24,* 461-474.

Oliver, R. T. (1971). *Communication and Culture in Ancient India and China.* Syracuse, NY: Syracuse University Press.

Oxford English dictionary. (1989) Clarendon Press; Oxford: New York; Oxford University Press

Pepper, G. L. (1995). *Communicating in Organizations: Cultural Approach.* New York: McGraw-Hill.

Pye, L. W. (1988). *The Mandarin and the Cadre: China's Political Cultures.* Ann Arbor, MI: Center for Chinese Studies, University of Michigan.

Rice, R. and Katz, J. (2001). *The Internet and Health Communication: Experiences and Expectations.* Thousand Oaks, CA: Sage Publications, Inc.

Tan, J.K., and Benbasat, I. (1993). The effectivenss of graphical presentation for information. *Decision Sciences*, 24, 167-191.

Turoff, M., Chumer, M., Van De Walle, B., Yao, X. (2004). The design of a dynamic emergency response management information system (DERMIS). *Journal of Information Technology Theory and Application*, 5(4), 1-35.

Vessey, I. (1991). Cognitive fit: A theory-based analysis of the graphs versus. *Decision Sciences*, 22, 219-240.

Vessey, I., and Galletta, D.F. (1991). Cognitive fit: An empirical study of information acquisition. *Information Systems Research*, 2, 63-84.

Wilcox, D. L., Ault, P. H. and Agee, W. K. (1995). *Public Relations: Strategies and Tactics.* New York: Harper Collins.

Yum, J. O. (1997). The impact of Confucianism on interpersonal relationships and communication patterns in East Asia. In L. A. Samovar and R. E. Porter (Eds.), *Intercultural Communication: A Reader* (8th ed., pp. 78-88). Belmont, CA: Wadsworth.

Yu, T. and Wen, W. C. (2003). Crisis communication in Chinese culture: A case study in Taiwan. *Asian Journal of Communication*, 13(2), 50-64.

In: Crisis Management in Chinese Contexts   ISBN: 978-1-61761-609-9
Editor: Zenbobia C. Y. Chan   © 2011 Nova Science Publishers, Inc.

Chapter 2

CRISIS MANAGEMENT FOR FINANCIAL TSUNAMI VICTIMS

Zenobia C. Y. Chan[1] and Wing-Fu Lai[2]

[1] School of Nursing, The Hong Kong Polytechnic University
[2] University of Hong Kong, Faculty of Science

SUMMARY

Financial tsunami is a current global crisis, and has been devastatingly impacting on the global economies since it started in the U.S. Due to its influences on areas ranging from economics to the health quality of the public, proper crisis management is imperative. Over the years, though financial measures to cope with the recession have been widely discussed in the commercial, public and political sectors, little discussion has been made from the social work perspective. In this chapter, we are going to explore potential health links between the tsunami and individuals in the society, and ponder its implications on social work practices for the victims so that more holistic care can be provided to those suffering from the economic depression.

OVERVIEW

Using C. Wright Mills' insightful thesis of 1959, the distinction between "personal troubles of milieu" and "public issues of social structure" lets us understand how individuals interact with the environment, and how the environment shapes individual lives. Therefore, it is worthy to explore possible health links between the current financial tsunami and individuals, and the practices of crisis management in the context of social work.

The financial tsunami, which has been simmering for over a year due to toxic debts and extreme over-leveraging in giant investment banks in the U.S., is one of the most influential global crises of recent decades. Since the recession started in the U.S. in September 2008, its shockwaves have quickly inundated the global economies. Though measures to combat the tsunami have been extensively discussed in the commercial, public and political sectors, little discussion has been made on the health aspect and crisis management of the issue from the social work perspective. Crisis management is an approach to tackling emergency, in which proper preparation, time management, timing, communication and coordination are imperative. It is hoped that this chapter can raise the awareness of management practices in the social work and healthcare contexts for future financial crises.

IMPLICATIONS FOR SOCIAL WORK PRACTICES

Economic crises are an important topic as far as crisis management is concerned. This is because such crises can usually have a great impact on health outcomes. This is exemplified by the increase in the mortality rate in Mexico (Cutler, et al. 2002), and the worsening of infant mortality in Latin America and the Caribbean during the economic recession of the 1980s (Musgrove, 1987). As delineated in *The Times* by Byron in September 2008 (Byron, 2008), the psychological burden caused by the financial tsunami on people can be as heavy as the financial loss. This can be shown in Hong Kong, where more than 1,000 people have sought counseling for emotional problems via the governmentally-financed 24-hour hotline services. Many of the cases received are seen to be retired old people, middle class and even the rich people. In view of such reality, what are the implications to social work practices for financial tsunami victims?

First of all, the victims may have endured different levels of hardship in the tsunami. Therefore, the first level of crisis management adopted by social workers is to be alerted to the victims' economic risks and negative emotions (such as hopelessness, anger, depression, anxiety and emotional instability) and to recognize the potential links between their psychological distress and the tsunami. With the trend of adopting the evidence-based approach in contemporary social work practices (Zlotnik et al., 2004), social workers are encouraged to make good use of the convergence of the explosion of information technology, research databases, and empirically based service models of decision making in interventions adopted to address the needs of individual clients. In addition, they may also follow the five major steps below for the delivery of evidence-based social work services for management of economic crises (Gossett et al., 2007):

1) Formulation of answerable questions based on clients' needs
2) Collection of proper external evidence to tackle the questions
3) Evaluation of collected evidence
4) Adoption of the evaluation in decision making
5) Provision of intervention

In addition to the aforementioned, as economic crisis is known to have great psychosocial impact on the society (Waters, et al. 2003; Yang, et al. 2001), the second level of crisis management adopted by social workers is to receive psychiatric training so that they are capable of differentiating psychological symptoms from disorders. As certain negative emotions like depression and anxiety can either routinely appear in everyday life or be manifestations of more severe mental and physical problems, a basic understanding of the diagnostic threshold and proper evaluation of the necessity for further referral to specialized centers would be required among social workers. The efficiency of crisis management will be largely influenced by the timing of actions; therefore, no hesitation should be made in cases where further referral of clients to advanced health professional is deemed necessary. Furthermore, because sometimes life stress may just manifest as physical symptoms (such as chest pain, dizziness, nausea, weight loss, palpitations and insomnia), it is important for those symptoms and the underlying psychological constraints to be identified.

To holistically accommodate the needs of the victims of the financial tsunami, provision of psychological and physical assessments is legitimate. Much more than that, however, is the necessity of having the third level of crisis management adopted by social workers to cope with economic crises among victims, i.e., the presence of a global sense of the current affairs, the abilities to evaluate the victims' social needs, and the proficiency of assessing the vulnerability of the victims to financial pressure. Attention should be paid not only to affected investors, but also to those non-investing community members who may be victimized because of the side-effects (such as unemployment) of the tightened lending standards and the shrunken global market. Such legitimacy is exhibited by the United Nations' International Labour Organization, which projected that global unemployment may increase up to 210 million people by the end of 2009. This change in the social employment pattern can deleteriously affect not only personal finance, but also household incomes.

As suggested by Hopkins in his review summarizing the observation of the health status changes in Indonesia, Malaysia and Thailand during the 1990s economic crisis in East Asia (2006), the budgetary pressure on personal and household finance may cause the following social distress: poverty, cutbacks on food or substitution with less nutritional food, and reductions in primary health care consumption. The latter has been supported by earlier research conducted by Yang's group (2001), who identified the reciprocal relationship between household health expenditures and family incomes via analyzing the urban household income-expenditure survey data, national health insurance claims data, and public health centre surveys collected during the severe economic recession in Korea in the 1990s. Similar changes in health care utilization were also reported in Indonesia during the 1997-98 East Asian economic crisis (Waters, et al. 2003). In addition to those aforementioned, financial crises may also lead to social problems such as social withdrawal, family conflicts or even violence; all these factors may link to psychological and/or physical problems discussed above. Social workers, policy makers and other professionals ought to be alert of such facts. They should collaborate to formulate proper management plans for the crisis and provide professional interventions to the victims in a timely basis.

CONCLUDING REMARKS

As the financial tsunami is a global socio-political issue, the affected victims and their families may experience both psychological and social needs. Social workers should adopt proper crisis management measures and be sensitive to the influence of the social affairs on the clients' needs. Instead of merely confronting the financial concerns, it is also important for them to care for their clients' psychosocial dimension. If necessary, referring the subjects in need to other professional bodies in the medical, financial and social fields for further follow-up may be required so that a partnership approach between different professions can be promoted. Such collaboration is an important part of the crisis management plan, in which genuine interdisciplinary cooperation and communication may be the only way to combat such a global hard times in the future.

THE SECOND AUTHOR'S BACKGROUND

Wing-Fu Lai graduated from the University of Hong Kong with a bachelor's degree in food and nutritional science. He was on the Dean's Honors List 2005/06 and 2006/07 of the Faculty of Science, and is currently pursuing a Ph.D. degree in chemical biology. He can be contacted at rori0610@graduate.hku.hk.

REFERENCES

Byron, T. (2008 September 17). Who suffers-and how the family can survive. *Times*, Sect 4.

Cutler, D. M., Knaul, F., Lozano, R., Mendez, O., & Zurita, B. (2002). Financial crisis, health outcomes, and aging: Mexico in the 1980s and 1990s. *Journal of Public Economics*, *84*(2): 279-303.

Gossett, M., & Weinman, M. L. (2007). Evidence-based practice and social work: an illustration of the steps involved. *Health & Social Work, 32*(2), 147-150.

Hopkins, S. (2006). Economic stability and health status: evidence from East Asia before and after the 1990s economic crisis. *Health Policy, 75*(3):347-57.

Mills, C. W. (1959). *The Sociological Imagination*. New York: OUP.

Musgrove, P. (1987). The economic crisis and its impact on health and health care in Latin America and the Caribbean. *International Journal of Health Services, 17*(3):411-441.

Waters, H., Saadah, F., & Pradhan, M. (2003). The impact of the 1997-98 East Asian economic crisis on health and health care in Indonesia. *Health Policy Plan, 18*(2):172-181.

Yang, B.M., Prescott, N., & Bae, E.Y. (2001). The impact of economic crisis on health-care consumption in Korea. *Health Policy Plan, 16* (4):372-385.

Zlotnik, J. L., & Galambos, C. (2004). Evidence-based practices in health care: social work possibilities. *Health & Social Work, 29*(4), 259-261.

In: Crisis Management in Chinese Contexts   ISBN: 978-1-61761-609-9
Editor: Zenbobia C. Y. Chan   © 2011 Nova Science Publishers, Inc.

Chapter 3

THE CRISIS MANAGEMENT OF SCHOOL IN HUMAN SWINE INFLUENZA OUTBREAK

Tony C.M. Lau[1] and Zenobia C. Y. Chan[2]

[1] Head of Moral and Civic Education Committee in a Secondary School
[2] School of Nursing, The Hong Kong Polytechnic University

SUMMARY

The outbreak of human swine influenza (HSI) in different areas in 2009 aroused concern throughout the world. In order to combat this disease's transmission, various health organizations have tried their best to set up special crisis management teams to deal with the effects in the community. Since schools are places that gather many students, teachers and parents, they are the high-risk groups to contract the HSI virus. We must be on alert and strengthen personal and environmental hygiene. In a school setting, an effective crisis management team is essential to formulate preventive and contingency measures against HSI. In this paper, the role of the school crisis management team, the response mechanism and post-event evaluation will be the key issues to be emphasized. The hierarchy of the crisis management team and the roles of different crisis management team members are taken from one secondary school used as an example. Different schools may have their own makeup of staff, students, parents and surrounding community, so the information or reviews in this paper can serve as a reference for the

---

[1] E-mail: tonylau516@yahoo.com.hk

schools towards disease prevention. Many in-depth studies, in areas such as teacher training, rehearsal practice or resource allocation, should be investigated in the future.

INTRODUCTION

From the past experiences of disease outbreak in the community, such as SARS (severe acute respiratory syndrome) and avian influenza, the crisis management is not so effective and creates many problems in the communication and intervention. The 2003 SARS in Hong Kong constituted an acute emergency for the Hong Kong government, because local and international public safety was at great risk. However, the Hong Kong government's crisis management for SARS was considered the worst among its other counterparts (Cheng, 2004). The Hong Kong government's image and reputation were affected as local citizens and media accused it of being "impotent" in handling the crisis. There is a pressing need to understand the dynamics of crisis situations as this may help with proper prevention, preparation and response. It does not focus on ad hoc improvisation; as such response does not appear acceptable for stakeholders and the general public in the current era.

Crisis Management involves prevention, intervention and evaluation. Many organizations or school settings only focus on prevention, but lack support in intervention and evaluation. Once a certain kind of crisis happens, they find that the most difficult part is the intervention, i.e. what to do during and immediately after a crisis. Different crises, such as suicide, natural disasters or disease outbreak, have their own characteristics. Every school is unique in its makeup of staff, students, parents and surrounding community. In order to deal with the crisis in the most effective way, it is essential to build up a comprehensive management system.

Nowadays, different kinds of disease outbreak threaten the community, especially in a school setting, where a lot of students, teachers and parents are disturbed. If there is a certain kind of disease outbreak, such as human swine influenza (HSI), school routines will be greatly disrupted. In order to maintain stability in a school once a crisis has happened, the school has to activate the crisis management procedures to minimize the disturbance and handle the enquiries from its various stakeholders and the mass media efficiently. The ultimate goals are to resume the normal functioning and redress equilibrium of the school. In this paper, I would like to emphasize the role of the school in

HSI outbreak, especially the response mechanism, and the role of a crisis management team in a school. Besides, I will also focus on the pre-event action, ongoing action and post-event action taken to deal with disease outbreak. The most important part is the evaluation of the event and formulating a proper and effective response mechanism to various kinds of disease outbreak in the future.

LITERATURE REVIEW

Reported Cases of Swine Flu Viral Infection

The outbreak of HSI began in 2009. The disease was first detected in April 2009 in California (USA) and then migrated to other parts of the Americas, Europe, Australia, and Asia. Swine flu is a 'triple-reassortment" influenza virus, containing genes from human, swine and avian influenza A viruses. As of August 19, 2009, 210 countries have officially reported over 182,166 cases of swine flu viral infection, including 1,799 deaths reported by over 40 countries. The United States has reported the majority of fatal cases: 7,511 laboratory-confirmed human cases, including 477 deaths. The other countries reporting laboratory-confirmed cases include Mexico, Canada, the United Kingdom, Australia, Thailand, Chile, Spain, Panama, Brazil, and India. On April 29, 2009 the World Health Organization designated the outbreak a pandemic (Manish Sinha, 2009).

Potential Dangers of Human Swine Influenza

People of any age with certain chronic medical conditions, children less than 5 years of age, people 65 or older, and pregnant women might be at an increased risk for complications from swine flu viral infection (Jamieson, Honein, Rasmussen, Williams, Swerdlow and Biggerstaff et al., 2009). Unlike typical influenza seasonal outbreaks, the percentage of patients infected with swine flu requiring hospitalization (2–6%) appears to be higher than would be expected during a typical influenza season (0.4–1%) (Stamboulian, Bonvehí, Nacinovich and Cox, 2000). Besides, the need for hospitalization for swine flu viral infection has been particularly high among people between the ages of 1.5 and 59 years (Shinde, Bridges, Uyeki, Shu, Balish and Xu et al., 2009). Complications like pneumonia and dehydration have required hospitalization in approximately 2–5% of confirmed cases in the United States and 5–6% in Mexico (Chowell, Miller and Viboud, 2009). Asian countries have reported

106 deaths. Europe and Africa have reported fewer deaths. As of May 29, 2010, the Centre for Health Protection (CHP) had recorded a total of 80 fatal cases since May 1, 2009. They were 56 males and 24 females, with ages ranging from 1 to 95 years (median: 56 years).

In a school setting, students, teachers and school staff are the high-risk groups for HSI infection. This virus can spread rapidly through sustained human-to-human transmission, such as inhalation of infectious droplets and droplet nuclei, and by direct contact, which is facilitated by air and land travel and social gatherings. The most frequently reported symptoms are fever, cough, myalgia, and sore throat. Since students have many social gatherings and always study in a classroom, they have a greater chance to suffer from this kind of disease. How to minimize the number of infections of swine flu in a school is the most important point to discuss and with which to be concerned. Hence, a mechanism for rapid crisis management response to disease outbreak should be essential for a school setting.

Definition of Crisis Management

The concept of crisis management has seen a steady evolution over the last 20 years. Early phases of this evolution included Littlejohn's (1983, p. 13) six step crisis model (structure design, crisis team selection, team training, crisis situation audit, contingency plan, manage the crisis); *Fink, 1986 S. Fink, Crisis management: Planning for the inevitable, American Management Association, New York (1986);* Fink's seminal (1986, pp. 21–25) four stage model (prodromal, acute, chronic, resolution); Burnett's (1998, p. 482) 16-cell classification matrix approach; and the Home Office (UK) Emergency Planning College eight stage planning process (direction, information gathering, plan writing, consultation, publication, training validation, confirmation/revision—Harrison, 1999, p. 21). The "crisis" phenomena may be viewed in different ways by different actors, but the general idea about crisis management is characterized by three sets of conditions: severe and largely unexpected threats, high uncertainty, and the need for urgency in decision making (Rosenthal et al., 2001; Boin et al., 2005). From the experience of SARS, avian influenza and HSI outbreaks in Hong Kong, the main focus of crisis management should be the preparedness for the disease outbreak and the immediate actions taken to cope with these unexpected events. The logic of crisis management is that we need to give serious consideration to strong, well-resourced and forward thinking contingency planning if we want to tame and gain control over a crisis when it hits (Nudell and Antokol, 1988; Seymour and Moore, 2000; Mitroff, 2001; Boin et al., 2005). A comprehensive crisis management strategy for HSI outbreak in a school setting will be discussed in this paper so as to arouse the public awareness of the need of well-developed crisis management plans in a society.

ACTION TAKEN

Crisis Management Team Establishment

In order to effectively and efficiently respond to disease outbreak in a community, such as a school setting, a crisis management team should be established. This team should comprise a group of school staff that knows the school environment, the students, the parents and each other well enough to make the necessary decisions when a crisis, such as HSI outbreak, occurs. The main goals of the crisis management team are to maintain the safety, stability and consistency of a school. This team should be able to perform the following functions so as to manage all the positive or negative effects of a crisis and to help the school restore its normal routine functioning:

- Construct a comprehensive crisis management plan.
- Collect and clarify the crisis information regularly.
- Evaluate the impact of the crisis on the school.
- Coordinate all the resources in response to the crisis.
- Provide suitable support and guidelines for teaching and non-teaching staff, students and parents.
- Formulate the structure and progress of the crisis management.
- Respond effectively to the mass media.
- Evaluate the crisis management plan from time to time.
- Organize appropriate rehearsal for certain kinds of crisis response.
- Coordinate the follow up work.
- (School crisis management suggestion, Education Bureau)

For the HSI outbreak in the community, the school crisis management team should be activated to respond to the effects of the disease and provide appropriate support and guidelines for the teachers, students and parents, in order to prevent the infection of the disease.

The Hierarchy of the Crisis Management Team:

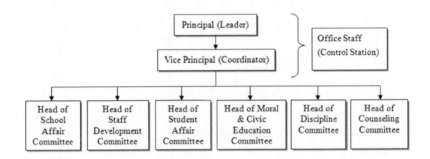

Apart from different members' duties, it is necessary to design a complete crisis response flow chart for the systematic coordination of all crisis intervention.

The Roles Of Different Team Members

Team member	Roles
Principal	✧ Acts as the team leader and coordinates the crisis response. ✧ Oversees the crisis management (e.g. swine flu information and number of infection cases). ✧ Makes important decisions in handling crisis (including the response to mass media). ✧ Conducts evaluation of the crisis management plan.
Vice Principal	✧ Facilitates the decisions made by the principal. ✧ Coordinates the duties assigned to different team members. ✧ Acts as a bridge to coordinate all the resources and regularly reports the progress of the management plan to the principal.
Head of School Affair Committee	✧ Evaluates the impact of disease outbreak on the school. ✧ Communicates with the Centre for Health Protection (CHP) and Education Bureau (EDB) District Office to obtain up-to-date information about the HSI infection and the proper action taken by the school. ✧ Prepares a press release to the mass media. (If certain students are infected with HSI, class suspension should be implemented and information about the arrangements needs to be announced to the public.)
Head of Staff Development	✧ Coordinates the support for teaching and non-teaching staff in handling the crisis.

Committee	✧ Prepares list of student names and telephone numbers for all class teachers to use to communicate with the parents during the time of suspension, if class suspension need to be implementedArranges and assists in conducting staff briefing and debriefing.
Head of Student Affair Committee	✧ Monitors the number of student absence cases during the outbreak of swine flu. ✧ Disseminates up-to-date information about HSI to students. ✧ Coordinates the communication with parents. ✧ Coordinates with outside resources to provide support to school, staff and students.
Head of Moral & Civic Education Committee	✧ Promotes health education in school. ✧ Reminds students about the personal hygiene and the attitudes towards disease outbreak. ✧ Prepares teaching materials about HSI and handling techniques for the class teachers to conduct a special assembly for the students.

Crisis Management Response Flow Chart

Pre-event Action

Disaster-management planning and rehearsal are believed to reduce morbidity and mortality in the event of a disaster. Proper planning and rehearsal reduce stress by providing participants with a sense of control and the effect extends throughout the event (Schouten, Callahan, and Shannon, 2004).

In a school setting, the crisis management team needs to develop guidelines for all teachers and staff to prepare for a crisis outbreak, such as SARS, HSI or hand-foot-mouth disease. Schools have the responsibility to maintain a better hygienic environment for staff and students. There is a class suspension mechanism for all schools in Hong Kong if certain kinds of transmissible disease outbreak becomes popular and threatens students' health. This mechanism is managed by the Centre for Health Protection and Education Bureau. Take HSI as an example; all schools need to pay attention to the trend of this disease outbreak in the community. For example, Perry and Lindell (2003) suggest that pre-crisis planning processes should:

a) be based on accurate knowledge of threats and likely human responses.
b) encourage appropriate action by crisis managers.
c) encourage flexibility in responses.
d) promote inter-organizational coordination.
e) integrate plans for each hazard into a multi-hazard approach.
f) involve the training of relevant personnel.
g) provide for testing through drills and exercises.
h) be adaptable as part of an ongoing process to adjust to new circumstances.
i) be a strong advocate in the face of inevitable resistance to resource commitments for low probability events.
j) recognize the differences between crisis planning (preparedness) and crisis management (implementation and performance).

The crisis management team of a school should be kept abreast of the latest developments and pay attention to the online news and information of EDB and CHP. Such teams should plan and manage matters relating to the prevention of HSI, e.g. briefings for staff and students on knowledge about swine flu, daily precautionary measures, contingency measures for when students have contracted the disease, etc. Furthermore, setting up a communication mechanism, and the allocation of human and financial resources are very important in the pre-event action. All school staff, students and parents should be informed of the arrangements. Civic Education and parents' participation are both important in the prevention of contracting the swine flu virus. It should be emphasized to students that everyone in the community bears the responsibility for preventing the spread of the disease. The Moral and Civic Education Committee should explain to parents in detail the symptoms of HSI and urge them to keep an eye on their children's health condition.

On-going eEent Action

If a student in a school is confirmed to have contracted HSI or students and staff have close contact with HSI cases, CHP and EDB may request that the school suspends classes so as to prevent the spread of the disease. Therefore, some measures need to be taken by school:

a) The crisis management team should be activated immediately to plan and handle various arrangements relating to class suspensions and to discuss the contingency plans in case of an extension of the class suspension period.

b) The team should keep in contact with EDB and CHP and follow their instruction.

c) Circulars about the arrangements of class suspension due to HSI should be prepared and distributed to students and parents.

d) The school has the responsibility to disseminate the message to parents that class suspension is a preventive measureaimed to reduce social contact so as to reduce the spread of HSI, keep parents alert at all times, and strengthen personal as well as environmental hygiene. Parents should keep an eye on the health condition of their child. If their child is found to have symptoms like fever, coughing, or sore throat, they should take their child to the Designated Flu Clinics (DFC) of the Hospital Authority (HA) for a medical check. Such action and information giving can relieve the anxiety among parents.

e) Any news concerning the school should be disseminated via the school intranet and website. Detailed guidelines about the prevention of the spread of HSI should be distributed to parents.

f) In order to meet practical needs during the class suspension, school should arrange a large scale clean up and disinfect the school premises.

g) An effective communication mechanism should be in place during the class suspension period. A suitable number of staff should be assigned to handle school affairs and answer parents' and students' enquiries about the latest arrangements and assignments. Besides, a press release draft should be prepared in case of the emergency situation and deal with the enquiries from the mass media immediately.

h) An effective reporting mechanism should also be set up during the class suspension period. The school has the responsibility to report to CHP and EDB about the number of staff and/or students confirmed or suspected of having contracted HSI.

The crisis management team in a school should play an important role in coordinating all the steps (a-h) mentioned above during the disease outbreak. However, the most important is the effective communication between school, parents, EDB and CHP. If all parties can perform well in their duties, the crisis management response can be done effectively and efficiently.

Post-event Action

Evaluation of the action plan is the best preparation for the future planning and preview of different types of crisis management. Based upon the experience of action taken in the HSI outbreak in the community and school settings, an effective communication plan is very important when the crisis happens. Checklists and phone trees are essential for the action to be taken to deal with different crises when they happen.

a. Checklists for Crisis Management Team

Different checklists should be prepared for different team members in the crisis management team. Different team members, such as Vice-principal, Head of School Affair, Student Affair, Moral and Civic Education, Staff Development and Office have to follow the items on the checklist and finish the tasks on time. The time frame is very important when dealing with different tasks in crisis management so as to prevent any delay in the plan's implementation.

b. Phone Tree for Immediate Communication

The purpose of preparing a phone tree is to communicate with people affected by a crisis. In the event of class suspension due to HSI, phone lists of students, parents, staff, the EDB Regional office, CHP, Department of Health, designated clinics, hospitals, school supervisors and the Incorporated Management Committee should be prepared immediately after the activation of the crisis management team in a school. This phone tree enables a message to be given quickly, personally and specially. This can also eliminate the anxiety of team members and save time when handling the crisis as all the information is already prepared and ready to use.

DISCUSSION

The effectiveness of the crisis management plan must be dependent on the effective cooperation between different members on the crisis management team. The principal acts as the leader and the Vice-principal acts as the coordinator in the crisis response plan. Monitoring of the progress of the response plan is also very crucial to the success of the implementation. In a school setting, there are also some limitations and improvement needs to be concerned when handling disease outbreak in the society. Even when the school has a well-organized crisis management team, parental support is also very important. However, it is difficult to ensure parents can follow all the instructions from school, EDB or CHP, such asensuring personal hygiene and keeping an eye on their children's health. Parent education should be focused on more, especially workshops or seminars organized by the Parent-Teacher-Association of the school.

The teacher's experience in crisis management is also another challenge of a school. Sometimes schools are more focused on academic, then there is less of a chance of crisis handling practice. Once a crisis happens, the vice-principal and the crisis management team need to coordinate all the manpower and resources to tackle the problem. Therefore, suitable levels of training or rehearsal should be provided for all teaching and non-teaching staff. They must, at least, have the concept of integrated communication, especially in front of the mass media. Due to the limited resources, full scale rehearsal may not be available for all schools, but table-top exercises can be arranged for the staff during the staff development days in a year.

The alertness of the school about disease outbreak should be raised in the new era. Based upon experiences in dealing with SARS, avian influenza and HSI, all private and public organizations, schools and households need to formulate a well-developed crisis management plan to deal with new disease outbreaks, such as hand-foot-mouth disease or related transmissible diseases. And of course, all the management teams need to keep up-to-date on the information about the global disease outbreak provided by the Department of Health and CHP. The school head needs to remind staff and parents to browse EDB's homepage for further announcements.

CONCLUSION

A school is a place that is more susceptible to disease transmission, as students and staff often have close social gatherings and contact. Therefore, students and teachers are high-risk groups in transmissible disease outbreaks. In order to minimize the number of students or staff that contract certain kinds of transmissible diseases, such as SARS, avian influenza, HSI, and hand-foot-mouth disease, a comprehensive crisis response mechanism should be set up to deal with the disease crisis. In order to achieve this goal, an effective crisis management team is essential for a school to maintain the safety, stability and consistency of a school environment and to continue its routine management. A strong communication network is also very important in crisis management, especially the timing of the response and the time frame for all appropriate actions that have to be taken. Good cooperation with other social communities, such as EDB, CHP, and Department of Health, can minimize the negative effects of allocation of resources, as they have much support and guidance on disease prevention. Apart from the policies in a school on disease prevention, environmental hygiene and crisis management team establishment, parent and student education about disease prevention are also very important in the promotion of healthy lifestyle. Both organizational and individual supports are also crucial to the success of the crisis response mechanism in a school setting. Teacher training and rehearsal practice of the management of different types of crises would be the most important issues that have to be focused on in the future.

AUTHOR'S BACKGROUND:

Lau Chun Man, Tony graduated from The University of Hong Kong (BSc in Biology) and The Chinese University of Hong Kong (PGDE). I have one-year's experience working in a merchandising company and 9 years of teaching experience (2 years in a primary school and 7 years in a secondary school). I am now the Head of Moral and Civic Education Committee in a secondary school. E-mail: tonylau516@yahoo.com.hk

REFERENCES

Allison, G.T. (2004), Public and private management: Are they fundamentally alike in all unimportant aspects?. In: M. Shafritz, A.C. Hyde and S.J. Parkes, Editors, *Classics of public administration*, Wadsworth, Belmont, CA (2004), pp. 396–413.

AMA (2002), *Crisis management and security issues survey, August 2002.* American Management Association.

Burnett, J.J. (1998), A strategic approach to managing crises, *Public Relations Review* 24 (1998) (4), pp. 475–488.

Carter, W. N. (1991), Disaster management: A disaster manager's handbook, Asian Development Bank, Manila.

Centre for Health Protection (The Government of the Hong Kong Special Administrative Region), Available at: 【http://www.chp.gov.hk/】.

Cheng, A. (2004), SARS in the storm, TOM Publishing Limited, Hong Kong.

Chowell, G., Miller, M.A. and Viboud, C. (2007), Seasonal influenza in the United States France and Australia: transmission and prospects for control, *Epidemiol Infect* 136, pp. 852–864.

Coburn, B.J., Wagner, B. G. and Blower, S. (2009), Modeling influenza epidemics and pandemics: insights into the future of swine flu (H1N1), *BMC Med* 7, p. 30.

Coombs, W.T. (2002), Deep and surface threats: Conceptual and practical implications for crisis vs. problem, *Pubic Relations Review* 28 (4), pp. 339–345.

Department of Health (The Government of the Hong Kong Special Administrative Region), Available at: 【http://www.dh.gov.hk/】.

Education Bureau (The Government of the Hong Kong Special Administrative Region), Available at: 【http://www.edb.gov.hk/】.

Fink, S. (1986), Crisis management: Planning for the inevitable, American Management Association, New York.

Guth, G.W. (1995), Organizational crisis experience and public relations roles, *Public Relations Review* 21 (1995) (2), pp. 123–136.

Harrison, S. (1999), Disasters and the media: Managing crisis communication, Macmillan, Basingstoke.

Heath, R.L. (1997), Strategic issues management: Organizations and public policy challenges, Sage, Thousand Oaks, CA.

Jamieson, D. J., Honein, M.A., Rasmussen, S.A., Williams, J.L., Swerdlow, D.L. and Biggerstaff, M.S. *et al.*, (2009) H1N1 influenza virus infection during pregnancy in the USA, *Lancet* 374 (2009), pp. 451–458.

Littlejohn, R.F. (1983), Crisis management: A team approach, AMA Management Briefing, New York.

Novel Swine-Origin Influenza A (H1N1) Virus Investigation Team, Emergence of a novel Swine-Origin Influenza A (H1N1) virus in humans, *N Engl J Med* 361 (2009), pp. 1–10.

Nudell, M. and Antokol, N. (1988), *The Handbook for Effective Emergency and Crisis Management*, Lexington Books, Lexington.

Penrose, J. (2000), The Role of Perception in Crisis Planning, *Public Relations Review* 26 (2000) (2), pp. 155–171.

Perez-Padilla, R., de la Rosa-Zamboni, D, Ponce de Leon, S, Hernandez, M, Quiñones-Falconi, F, and Bautista, E. (2009), Pneumonia and respiratory failure from Swine -Origin Influenza A (H1N1) in Mexico, *N Engl J Med* 361, pp. 680–689.

Perry, R.W. and Lindell, M. K. (2003), 'Preparedness for Emergency Response: Guidelines for the Emergency Planning Process', *Disasters, Volume 27*, Number 4, pp. 336-350.

Rosenthal, U., Boin, R.A. and Comfort, L. K. (2001), 'The Changing World of Crisis and Crisis Management', in Rosenthal, U., Boin, R. A. and Comfort, L. K. (Eds), *Managing Crises: Threats, Dilemmas and Opportunities*, Charles C. Thomas, Springfield, pp. 5 – 27.

Schouten, Ronald, Callahan, Michael V. and Bryant, Shannon. (2004), Community Response to Disaster: The Role of the Workplace, *Harvard Medical School; Department of Psychiatry and Centre for Integrating Medicine with Innovative Technology, Massachusetts General Hospital, Boston, MA; KeyPeople Resources, Inc.*

Shinde, V., Bridges, C.B., Uyeki, T.M., Shu, B., Balish, A. and Xu, X *et al.* (2009), Triple-reassortant swine influenza A (H1) in humans in the United States, 2005–2009, *N Engl J Med* 360, pp. 2616–2625.

Sinha, Manish. (2009), Swine Flu. *Journal of Infection and Public Health*, Volume 2, Issue 4, 2009, Pages 157-166.

Stamboulian, D., Bonvehí, P.E., Nacinovich, F.M. and Cox, N. (2000), Influenza, *Infect Dis Clin North Am* 14, pp. 141–166.

World Health Organization. Epidemic and Pandemic Alert and Response (EPR): Influenza A (H1N1)—update 62. Available at: http://www .who.int.easyaccess1.lib.cuhk.edu.hk/csr/don/2009_08_19/en/index.html; 2009 [accessed August 19, 2009].

In: Crisis Management in Chinese Contexts   ISBN: 978-1-61761-609-9
Editor: Zenbobia C. Y. Chan   © 2011 Nova Science Publishers, Inc.

Chapter 4

CRISIS MANAGEMENT IN PREVALENCE OF SEXUALLY TRANSMITTED DISEASES AMONG SECONDARY SCHOOL FEMALES

Mica S. F. Fong[1] and Zenobia C. Y. Chan

BA Arts (Hons.) PGDE (Chinese), Student of Master Programme of
Science in Health Education at The Chinese University of Hong Kong
School of Nursing, The Hong Kong Polytechnic University

SUMMARY

This chapter introduces crisis management in the prevalence of sexually transmitted diseases (STDs) among secondary school females by integrating both the current circumstances and current measures adopted for the prevention of infection by STDs among secondary school females. The foci of the exploration are the development of a plan for the prevention of infection by STDs among secondary school females and reflection on the possibility of implementing the crisis management plan for the issue concerned. To have an all-round probe into the issue, the preventive crisis management system and the information sharing system among organizations will be discussed.

[1] Email: tinnymica@yahoo.com.hk

INTRODUCTION

In recent years, the social problems caused by the changes of adolescents' attitudes towards sex are controversial issues in Hong Kong. Not astonishingly, the percentage of adolescents under age 16 who have experienced sexual intercourse increased drastically from 40.7% (Ho and Pun, 1997) to 77.7% (The Hong Kong Council of Social Service, 2008) between 1996 and 2008. The average age at which adolescents first experienced sexual intercourse also dropped from the age of 14.8 (Ho and Pun, 1997) to 14.4 (The Hong Kong Council of Social Service, 2008) between 1996 and 2008. This reveals that, nowadays, adolescents are more open-minded in respect of their attitudes towards sex.

The increase in the number of underage unplanned pregnancies caused by pre-marital intercourse, manslaughters caused by throwing new born babies of unplanned pregnancies, and the drastic increase in the number of adolescents infected by STDs reveal the inadequate crisis management of social problems aroused by the changes of adolescents' sexual attitudes. The social problems mentioned above, apart from STD infections, are systematically managed by governmental institutions and social organizations. For the infections related to STDs among adolescents, only non-preventive clinical services, such as biological checks and medications, are provided by the Department of Health when adolescents who suspect themselves of being infected by STDs seek help on their own initiative.

From 2006 to 2008, the number of adolescents under the age of 19 infected by STDs increased from 555 to 688 (The Department of Health of Hong Kong, 2008). This 24% increase shows the vigorous ascension of the number of adolescents under the age of 19 infected by STDs in these years. Regretfully, the prevalence of STDs among adolescents is left aside by the public and adolescents themselves.

In viewing the current circumstances of the sexual attitudes and behaviors of adolescents, the sexual attitudes of teenage females are relatively conservative; but the average frequency of sexual intercourse is obviously higher than that of their male counterparts. Most teenage girls first experience sexual intercourse without any reason, and the second most common reason is fulfilling their lovers' requests. Half of female teenagers believe that consecutive sexual intercourses could help keep a good boy-girl-relationship. Most probably, they are anxious about the result of unplanned pregnancies after sexual intercourse and safety measures adopted are mostly directed against pregnancies but not the infections to STDs. It is the reason why STDs are more prevalent among secondary school females in recent years.

It is worthwhile to go deep into the crisis management in the prevalence of STDs among secondary school females.

BACKGROUND LITERATURE

By reviewing the literature pertaining to crisis management and adolescents' attitudes towards sex, it is rare to discuss the crisis management strategies for prevention of STDs among secondary school females. Though there is lots of literature about the sex education needs of adolescents, the focus is mainly on the approaches of the curricula or young males' needs. Even in the field of crisis management, there is no specific model for the topic concerned.

Crisis is a vague concep, as its meaning can accord with one's definition. Frankly speaking, "a crisis has come to mean a moment of indecision, or the idea that something is not going well" (Carole Lalonde, 2004). Then, can crises be prevented? In respect of crisis management, it can be phased in three levels. The first level is the preventive phase; the second level is the emergency phase; and the third level is the consolidation and reconstruction phase (Chan, 2010). Different phases of crisis management are supported by various strategies, but the same principles of "good practices" apply. To fit in the reality, principles of "good practices" should be broad and movable (McConnell and Drennan, 2006).

Data and information sharing among the organizations involved in response to a specific crisis is crucial to the implementation of the crisis management plan. However, differences in organizational cultures, terminologies and incompatibility of standard operating procedures cripple the progress of data and information sharing among organizations (André Dantas & Erica Seville, 2006). To cope with the difficulties of sharing data and information among organizations, comprehensive analysis of the nature and background of involved organizations; the characteristics of their involvement; their data or information needs and sharing needs; and the ways for them to share data and information should be conducted (André Dantas & Erica Seville, 2006).

PREVENTIVE APPROACH OF CRISIS MANAGEMENT

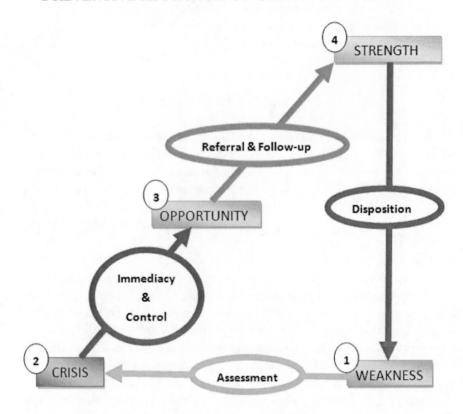

Figure 1. Model of Preventive Approach for Crisis Management.

The model above illustrates the preventive approach of crisis management. The processes are 1) identify the weaknesses of current circumstances for assessments of anticipated crisis; 2) reduce potential risk factors of anticipated crisis with immediacy and control measures; 3) refer high-risk cases to professionals with periodic follow-ups to strengthen the capability of resisting risk factors of crisis in the community; 4) pin the weaknesses of new circumstances by disposition. The model is a non-ended cycle which can modify the crisis management plan according to changes in circumstance.

PREVENTIVE APPROACH TO THE PREVALENCE OF STDS AMONG SECONDARY SCHOOL FEMALES

Step 1: Identification of the Weaknesses of Current Circumstances

By an overview of the current preventive system for the prevalence of STDs among adolescents, weaknesses are identified as follows:

- The sex education provided does not focus on female teenagers' needs.
- The current approach for coping with STDs is only clinical-based.
- There is inadequate support for schools, parents and social workers who handle adolescents perplexed by sex.
- There is no channel for adolescents to directly seek help when they suspect themselves of being infected by STDs.

In anticipation of the crisis being faced under the current circumstances, there need to be assessments of the sex education needs of female teenagers; the needs of schools, parents and social workers who may handle adolescents perplexed by sex; and the needs of adolescents who suspect themselves of being infected by STDs.

Step 2: Reduction to the Risk Factors of Anticipated Crisis

With the help of needs assessments in respect of the end-users, the following are risk factors of anticipated crisis:

- Female teenagers believe the misconception that "sexual intercourses can keep the harmony of boy-girl-relationship".
- There is low awareness of how to prevent STDs when teenagers choose contraceptive devices.
- Further infections will occur as teenagers know little about STDs.
- Teenagers may try to seek solutions from friends or the internet instead of seeking help from professionals when they suspect themselves of being infected by STDs.

Aimed at reducing the risk factors, sex education services tailor-made for teenage females will be provided; seminars about ways to handle adolescents perplexed by sex will be provided to schools, parents and social workers; holistic health surveys about sex education literacy and attitudes towards sex will be conducted periodically with secondary school students to find members at high-risk for the issue concerned; and hotlines for inquiry of suspected STDs infection cases will be set up. The above-mentioned immediacy and control measures play important roles in referring the high-risk cases to professionals for follow-ups.

Step 3: Strengthening of the Capability to Resist Risk Factors of Crisis in the Community

For high-risk members, referral and follow-up systems will be adopted to resist risk factors of becoming infected by STDs. Depending upon the different situations of high-risk members, they will be referred to council teachers, social workers, nurses, clinical psychologists, specialists in venereal diseases and so forth. Periodic follow-ups will be conducted to track the progress of their changes in sexual attitude and escalation of skills to keep healthy boy-girl-relationships, and rehabilitation from infections of STDs. With consecutive follow-ups, peoples' capability to resist risk factors of infection by STDs will be ultimately strengthened.

Step 4: Disposition for Weaknesses of New Circumstances

As surrounding circumstances change according to social factors, it is necessary to dispose of emerging weaknesses. To identify the emerging weaknesses, opinions should be sought from stakeholders of the prevention system being adopted. In respect of the prevention of STDs among secondary school females, stakeholders are: 1) services providers (such as the Department of Health), non-governmental organizations, secondary schools; 2) parents; and 3) secondary school females. Surveys and conferences can be conducted to collect useful information for further refinement of current system.

PLATFORM CENTRIC APPROACH OF INFORMATION SHARING SYSTEMS LEADS TO SUCESSFUL CRISIS MANAGEMENT PLANS

Needless to say, an effective and efficient data and information sharing system is the key to the success of a crisis management plan. For the platform centric approached information sharing system, an electronic data and information processing system is established for collecting data from and sharing information with inter-organizations involved in response to the incidents. A flood of redundant information may retard the action to the incident, therefore, the types of data being collected and information being shared are designated by the roles played by those inter-organizations.

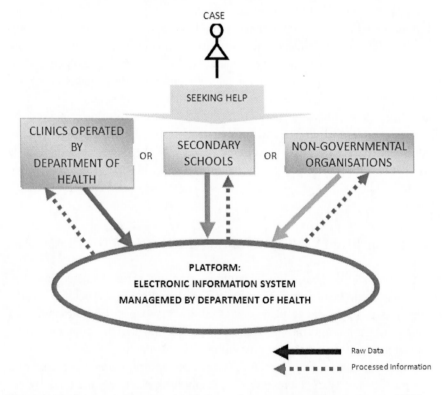

Figure 2: Platform centric approached information system for the prevalence of STDs among secondary school females.

Reviewing the current adopted system, the data and information sharing system is an end-user centric approach, which cripples inter-organizational cooperation to prevent the prevalence of STDs among secondary school females. There is no platform to share the data and information about adolescents perplexed by sexual issues among the clinics of the Department of Health, non-governmental organizations and secondary schools. Once a teenager is perplexed by sexual issues, only the party from whom he/she has sought help can grasp the useful information of the case. As those inter-organizations involved in responding to the cases are of different professional natures, decent measures may not be devoted to the crisis faced by the teenager. A platform centric approached data and information sharing system should be imposed to refine the system of referring high-risk students.

In the platform centric approached data and information sharing system, the Department of Health acts as a platform to collect data from and share information with clinics operated by the Department of Health, secondary schools attended by clients and non-governemental organizations in the community. According to the characters of these inter-organzations, information about psychological fluctuations and psychosocial conditions of the clients concerned will be shared with secondary schools attended by clients and non-governmental organizations in the community. Information about the physical condition of clients will be shared with the clinics to provide decent medication to the cases. To protect the privacy of the clients, information is only shared with professionals who handle the case, instead of with the whole organization.

POSSIBILITY OF IMPLEMENTATION OF THE PLAN

To evaluate the possibility of implementing any crisis management plan, indicators should be clearly defined. Many organizational stakeholders involve to the crisis management plan suggested in this paper. The flexibility of resource allocation and the integration of the organizational structure will be the indicators for evaluating the possibility of implementing such a plan.

Sufficient human and material resources can contribute to the success of a crisis management plan. Human resources emphasize not only the quantity but also the quality of manpower. Within the organization, reallocation of manpower based upon the staff's professions can reduce the cost of training manpower to operate on specific tasks. Training will only be adopted when there is insufficient manpower to support the tasks. Between the organizations involved, the division of tasks, based upon the professionals and the characteristics of manpower within organizations, can escalate the flexibility of resource allocation. The material resources act as instruments to facilitate the tasks of manpower. The platform centric approach for storage makes the allocation of material resources more flexible, as the platform coordinates the allotment of materials between organizations according to the tasks concerned.

Good inter-organizational structure is the only way to make resource allocation more elastic and smooth an implementation of a plan. The natures and backgrounds of organizations involved are quite different, forming their own cultures, administrative structures and information sharing systems. To cope with those differences crippling the communication between organizations, conferences for the administrative staff of those organizations involved should be held periodically to reconcile the discrepancies between them. For efficient information sharing among organizations involved, the platform centric approach of electronic data and information sharing system will be adopted. Organizations can share and collect information via the intranet by assigning authorizations to staff according to their functions.

Deeply looking into the plan…

Indicator 1: Flexibility of Resource Allocation

Clients are referred to council teachers, social workers, nurses, clinical psychologists, specialists in venereal diseases and so forth according to the different situations.As the division of tasks is coherent to the professional nature of the institutions, the quality of the human resources is high. For the allocation of the material resources, instruments needed by the organizations are quite different that needless to allot the resources by platform centric storage system. The flexibility of resources allocation of the plan is high.

Indicator 2: Integration to Organizational Structure

The platform centric approached data and information sharing system operated by the Department of Health is adopted to collect data from and share information among organizations. Information will be shared according to the inter-organizational criteria for follow-ups. In order to protect the privacy of clients, only those professionals handling their case will be able to access information from the sharing system. As surveys and conferences will be conducted for stakeholders, there are channels for organizations to reconcile their discrepancies by sharing their opinions and observations. The integration of organizational structure is efficient.

Under a holistic approach to both resource allocation systems and information sharing systems, the plan is possible to implement with the advocacy from the government.

CONCLUSION

The focal concerns of the principles of "good practices" of crisis management planning (Perry, R.W. & Lindell, M. K. 2003) are related to inter-organizational structure, information sharing system and human resources trainings. They imply the directions for inter-organizational structure, information sharing system and human resource trainings are correlated. Good uses of the linkage between these three main elements contribute to a practical and flexible crisis management plan.

Most probably, the design of the data and information sharing system departs from the inter-organizational structure. The only indicator for measuring the efficiency of a data and information sharing system is the speed at which messages pass between system users. The information sharing system can be advanced to process data collected according to the needs of different parties by using the linkage between the three main elements mentioned in the principles of "good practices" of crisis management planning,. Accurate and precise information provided by the system smoothens the operation of crisis management.

To return to this article, the model suggested can be adapted to all kinds of crisis management cases in the preventive phase. Identification of the weaknesses of current circumstances provides data for anticipating foreseeable risk factors for occurrences of crisis. A wise use of needs assessments for all stakeholders can prevent the misallocation of resources and escalate the efficiency with which risk factors are reduced. Throughout understanding to the culture differences between orgainsational stakeholders points out the direction to build up a holistic integrated orgainsational structure and information sharing system. A holistic integrated organizational structure and information sharing system can back up referrals and follow-ups for high-risk members. Consecutive assessments provide platforms to trace deficiencies to further develop preventive system. With the help of periodic conferences held to reconcile the discrepancies between organizational stakeholders, the redundancies in resource allocation and an inefficient flow of information can be avoided. Both the flexibility of resource allocation and integration of organizational structure are high. For the data and information sharing system, a platform is established for systematic processing of data collection and information is released according to the function of organizations. The linkage between inter-the organizational structure, information sharing system and human resources' training is tight. The plan is practical and efficient.

In conclusion, precise analyses of weaknesses of current circumstances, cultural differences between organizations involved, the data and information sharing system, and resource allocation establish a practical and efficient preventive crisis management plan.

AUTHOR'S BACKGROUND

Mica S.F. Fong, BA Arts (Hons.) PGDE (Chinese), Student of Master Programme of Science in Health Education at The Chinese University of Hong Kong. Email: tinnymica@yahoo.com.hk

REFERENCES

Adamson, Gary, Mcaleavy, Gerry, Donegan, Tony and Shevlin, Mark (2006). Teachers' perceptions of health education practice in Northern Ireland: reported differences between policy and non-policy holding schools. *Oxford Journal, Health Education Research, Vol 21, no.2 2006*, 113-120.

Bleakley, Amy, Hennessy, Michael and Fishbein, Martin (2006). Public Opinion on Sex Education in US Schools. *Arch Pediatr Adolesc Medical Journal, Vol 160*, 1151-1156.

Buston, Katie, Wight, Daniel, Hart, Graham and Scott, Sue (2002). Implementation of teacher-delivered sex education programme: obstacles and facilitating factors. *Oxford Journal, Health Education Research, Vol 17, no.1 2002*, 59-72.

Campos, David (2002). *Sex, Youth, and Sex Education: a reference handbook.*

Chi On Ho, Billy and Han PUN, Shuk (1997). *The Knowledge of and Attitude towards Aids-related Issues Among Marginal Youth.* CityU Consultants Ltd.

Dantas, André and Seville, Erica (2006). Organizational issues in implementing an information sharing framework: lessons from the Matata flooding events in New Zealand. *Journal of Contingencies and Crisis Management*, 14 (1), 38-52.

Henderson, M., Wight, D., Raab, G.M., Abraham, C., Parkes, A., Scott, S.and Hart, G. (2007). Impact of a theoretically based sex education programme (SHARE) delivered by teachers on NHS registered conceptions and terminations: final results of cluster randomised trial. *British Medical Journal 2007*, 334:133.

Lalonde, Carole (2004). In Search of Archetypes in Crisis Management. *Journal of Contingencies and Crisis Management Volume 12, Number 2*, 76-88.

Li, Shiung Fu (2001). *Ducks in turbulent waters: Situation and Needs Analysis of Hong Kong Secondary Schools in Implementing Sex Education.*

Lin, Siu Fung (2007). *Values & Attitudes of Adolescents on Sexual Behaviour and Sexual Education.*

McConnell, Allan and Drennan, Lynn (2006). Mission Impossible? Planning and Preparing for Crisis. *Journal of Contingencies and Crisis Management Volume 14, Number 2*, 59-70.

Mellanby, A.R., Newcombe, R.G, Rees, J. and Tripp, J.H. (2001). A Comparative Study of Peer-led and Adult-led School Sex Education. *Oxford Journal, Health Education Research, Vol 16, no.4 2001*, 481-492.

Mother's Choice (2009). *Press Release* on March 28, 2009. http://www.motherschoice.com/pages/index.asp?pg=about_us_media_bureau_news_clip

Schatz, Paulette, Dzvimbo, Kuzvinetsa P. (2001). The adolescent sexual world and AIDS prevention: a democratic approach to program design in Zimbabwe. *Oxford Journal, Health Education Research, Vol 16, no.2 2001*, 127-136.

Schouten, Ronald, Callahan, Michael V. and Bryant, Shannon (2004). Community Response to Disaster: The Role of the Workplace. *Harv Rev Psychiatry. July/August 2004*, 229-237.

Sexuality Information and Education Council of the United States (SIECUS) http://www.siecus.org/index.cfm

Shang, Wenjing and Hooker, Neal H (2005). Improving recall crisis management: should retailer information be disclosed? *Journal of Public Affair 5*, 329-341.

Strage, Vicki, Forrest, Simon and Oakley, Ann. The RIPPLE Study Team (2002). Peer-led sex education-characteristics of peer educators and their perceptions of the impact on them of participation in a peer education programme. *Oxford Journal, Health Education Research, Vol 17, no.3 2002 ,327-337.*

Sun Daily (2009). *Press Release* http://the-sun.on.cc/cnt/news/20090822/0 0407_023.html

The Education Bureau of Hong Kong Special Administrative Region-Curriculum Development.

The Hong Kong Council of Social Services (2008). *Press Release* http://www.hkcss.org.hk/cm/cc/press/detail.asp?id=294

Tzeng, Huey-Ming (2005). Crisis Management Policies and Programs to Prevent Nursing-Related Medical Disputes in Taiwanese Hospital. *Nursing Economic$, Volume 23, No.5,* 239-247.

Weitzman, Eben A. (2002). Responding to September 11: A Conflict Resolution Scholar / Practitioner's Perspective. *Analyses of Social Issue and Public Policy 2002,* 109-117.

Wellings, K., Wadsworth, J., Johnson, A.M, Field, J., Whitaker, L.and Field, B. (1995). Provision of Sex Education and Early Sexual Experience: the relation examined. *British Medical Journal 1995;311,* 417-420.
http://www.edb.gov.hk/index.aspx?nodeID=2365&langno=1

In: Crisis Management in Chinese Contexts   ISBN: 978-1-61761-609-9
Editor: Zenbobia C. Y. Chan   © 2011 Nova Science Publishers, Inc.

Chapter 5

CRISIS MANAGEMENT PLAN FOR MEDICATION INCIDENT IN AN ACUTE HOSPITAL

K. Y. Lam[1] and Zenobia C. Y. Chan[2]
[1] The Chinese University of Hong Kong
[2] School of Nursing, The Hong Kong Polytechnic University

SUMMARY

Crises happen in our everyday lives. They are unpredictable and inevitable. Good crisis management is able to turn danger into opportunity. Hospitals are places with various procedures that involve a wide range of people from different parts of the society. This makes hospital settings prone to patient safety crises. Medical incident is a hot issue in newspapers in Hong Kong nowadays. Among all, medication error is a major one. However, there is no well-documented and detailed crisis management plan for medication incidents in the hospitals. This chapter reviews literature related to crisis management and medication incidents. It presents a crisis management plan with reference to a case scenario of medication incident in an acute hospital. It aims to address the importance of medication safety and the nurses' responsibility in maintaining medication safety, to discuss current practices in the administration of medication, and to develop a crisis management plan

---

[1] E-mail: teresalam@yahoo.com

for medication incidents in local hospitals. It also discusses the implications of the crisis management plan for future practice.

INTRODUCTION

Crises happen in our everyday lives and have been occurring forever (Devlin, 2007). They are unpredictable and inevitable (Chan, 2009), and they can occur anywhere at anytime (Spillan, 2003). They can come in the forms of natural disasters, terrorist attacks, outbreaks of infectious diseases, or other sudden events happening on the community and individual level. There will be a wide range of negative consequences if crises are not managed effectively and efficiently. Thus, planning and preparing for crisis is crucial and should be high on institutional and policy agendas (McConnell and Drennan, 2006).

The hospital setting is a place that deals with life and death issues. Various procedures, of different levels of complexity, take place in the hospitals, which involve people from different parts of the society. Such an environment makes hospitals more prone to crisis. Nowadays, news related to medical incidents such as wrong site surgery, patient suicide, wrong identification of patients and retaining of instruments in patients' bodies, etc. is no longer something unfamiliar to people in Hong Kong. Among all the medical incidents, improper administration of medications is one of the major areas of medical error (Chan, 2006). Although a Medication Safety Committee was established by the Hospital Authority (HA) to develop and implement projects for safer handling of drugs in the public hospitals (HA, 2008), there is no crisis management plan specific to medication incidents. A detailed and effective crisis management plan for medication incidents for the hospitals in Hong Kong is needed.

This paper has three objectives: 1) to address the importance of medication safety and the nurses' responsibility in maintaining medication safety; 2) to discuss current practices for administration of medication; and 3) to develop a crisis management plan for medication incidents in local hospitals. It begins with a review of literature related to crisis management and medication incidents. It is followed by a crisis management plan for medication incidents in an acute hospital with reference to a case scenario. It ends with a discussion on the implications for future crisis management.

LITERATURE REVIEW

Crisis and Crisis Management

Covello (1995) defined crisis as an unplanned event that triggers a real, perceived, or possible threat to safety, health, the environment, or to an organizations' reputation and credibility (as cited in Chan, 2009). Crisis events have a low probability of occurring, are usually unexpected, can be highly damaging and require quick and decisive action (Parnell, Koseoglu and Spillan, 2010). Crisis has increased in diversity and complexity in today's world (Rosenthal, Boin and Comfort, 2001, as cited in Lalonde, 2007). Examples include natural disasters (floods, tornadoes and earthquakes), terrorist attacks (the World Trade Centre attacks of September 11, 2001), outbreaks of infectious diseases (SARS and avian flu), and organizations experiencing an unstable time (unintentional product contamination, product failure and financial problems) (Devlin, 2007; Parnell et al., 2010; McConnell and Drennan, 2006; Koster and Politis-Norton, 2004).

Crisis management refers to the special measures taken to solve problems caused by a crisis (Devlin, 2007). It seeks to minimize the impact that crises bring to organizations (Parnell et al., 2010). It can handle sudden tragedy, minimize life-threatening effects and control the progress of damage (Chan, 2009). The ability to manage crisis successfully can mean the difference between survival and disaster (Spillan, 2003). Crisis can be a turning point, presenting both danger and opportunity (Hoff, Hallisey and Hoff, 2009). Good crisis management should maximize every opportunity (Devlin, 2007). It brings out the positive aspects of crisis, which include testing limits, igniting potentialities and acknowledging limitations (Chan, 2009). In contrast, a failure in responding to crisis may result in erosion of reputation, system breakdown, creation of chaos and crises with far-reaching consequences and uncontrollable outcomes (Koster and Politis-Norton, 2004; Farazmand, 2007).

A hospital is a potential place for a patient safety crisis to occur (Wong and Chan, 2009). It was estimated that adverse outcomes occur in around 10% of admissions in the United Kingdom (Hoyle, 2005a), and between 44,000 and 98,000 patients in the United States die every year as a result of medical error (Flanagan, Nestel and Joseph, 2004). These not only cost the health service extra budget, but also bring loss of trust by patients and society and diminish satisfaction for patients and healthcare professionals (Bowen, Bitz and Benner, 2010). Patient safety is fundamental to healthcare professional practice and is a common goal within the healthcare sector (Flanagan et al., 2004). Good crisis management is essential in achieving such a goal.

Medication Incidents

Medication errors always rank high in number and severity among all medical incidents. It was estimated that more than 1.5 million people are harmed each year by medication errors in the United States (Jones and Treiner, 2010). Moreover, most incidents confirmed as leading to severe harm or death, in the United Kingdom in 2007, were caused by errors in drug administration (Warburton, 2010). Drug error is costly in terms of increased patients' length of stay, resources consumed, patient harm and lives lost (Webster and Anderson, 2002). It can also have devastating effects on staff (Fry and Dacey, 2007). Medication errors can occur at different stages of the medication use process, which includes prescribing, dispensing, administering and monitoring (Nguyen, Connolly and Wong, 2009). Medication administration is often regarded as the sharp edge in such process because errors from the prescribing and dispensing steps, if not intercepted, will result in the patient receiving the medication in error (Shane, 2009). It was reported that most medication errors occur at the point of administration, and administration errors rank third in the list of causes leading to loss of function or patient death (Pape, 2003, as cited in Emanuel and Pryce-Miller, 2009). Administration of medication (AOM) is primarily the responsibility of nurses, and it was claimed that nurses spend 40% of their time on this task (Shane, 2009). Although AOM is often viewed as a basic nursing task, it requires a complex interaction of a large number of specific decisions and actions (Emanuel and Pryce-Miller, 2009). The "5 Rights" is the golden rule for AOM: administer the right dose of the right medication through the right route to the right person at the right time (Malloch, Benner, Sheets, Kenward and Farrell, 2010). This principle is taught to nurses as part of their nursing education, but nurses may not always adhere to it (Shane, 2009). There are diverse factors leading to nurses doing wrong in AOM. For the personal factors, nurses may have inadequate knowledge or experience and poor mathematic competency (Emanuel and Pryce-Miller, 2009). They may be fatigued and have decreased concentration while performing AOM (Paparella, 2008). For the environmental factors, nurses may be distracted in an overcrowded ward with increased nursing activities and insufficient staffing (Paparaella, 2008a). Medication products with poor packaging and inadequate equipment also contribute to medication errors (Emanuel and Pryce-Miller, 2009). Furthermore, errors can come from unclear and illegible prescriptions and poor communication between nurses and doctors (Fry and Dacey, 2007; Nguyen et al., 2009).

In 2009, there were almost 1,600 medication incidents reported in all public hospitals in Hong Kong, and 42% of them involved administration errors (HA, 2009 and 2010a). Examples of these medication incidents are listed in Table 1. A Medication Safety Committee was established by the HA to promote safer handling of drugs through the issuance of updated guidelines and organization of training and sharing sessions with local and overseas experts (HA, 2008). It makes use of a medication incident reporting program bulletin as a risk management tool to safeguard patient safety (Ha, 2008). There was a 13% decrease in the number of medication incidents reported to HA in the year of 2008 and 2009 (HA, 2010b). However, medication incident is still a major local issue. A detailed and effective crisis management plan is needed to guide healthcare workers facing this patient safety crisis in order to minimize the harm to patients, staff, the hospital and the society.

Table 1. Examples of recent medication incidents in Hong Kong

Year	Mediation Incidents
2010	Oral hypoglycaemic agents were suspected of having been given to an old lady with no history of diabetes mellitus, and the lady developed severe hypoglycaemia during the hospital stay.
2009	Expired reconstituted BCG (Bacillus Calmette-Guerin) vaccine was injected into five newborns.
2009	Oral syrup morphine was given intravenously to a patient with cancer.
2009	Intravenous antibiotic was injected to the wrong baby due to identification error.

CASE SCENARIO

On an acute female orthopedic ward, two nurses were on the night shift, taking care of 36 patients. A 50-year-old lady with a left hip injury was found to have hypokalaemia after a blood test (plasma potassium level of 2.1 mmol/L). The on-call doctor was informed, and he prescribed a regimen of potassium supplements (Oral potassium chloride, 2 grams, three doses, every two hours; and Intravenous infusion of 20 mmol potassium chloride in 250 ml normal saline solution over two hours). The nurses followed the regimen and gave the oral potassium supplement as prescribed. However, no preparation of 20 mmol potassium chloride in 250 ml normal saline solution was available in the hospital. The nurses mistakenly gave half pint of 20 mmol potassium chloride in 500 ml normal saline solution to the patient and thought that it was of the right dose. The results from the blood test taken after the supplements were administered was available during the morning shift. The lady still had hypokalaemia (plasma potassium level of 2.9 mmol/L). The error was discovered by the ward manager during the morning shift. She queried about how the colleagues on the night shift could follow the intravenous regimen without getting emergency stock of concentrated potassium chloride to prepare the prescribed regimen.

In this case scenario, though the medication error was discovered in quite a short time, and there was no serious physical damage to the patient, it showed several problems. For example, the on-call doctor was not familiar with the medication preparation, and the nurse had inadequate mathematic competency. Furthermore, the ward manager needed to handle this incident. She needed to monitor the condition of the patient, to report the incident, to disclose to the patient and her relatives, to counsel the staff involved, and to evaluate the medication administration procedure, etc. There is no formal and detailed management plan to guide the ward manager in dealing with medication incidents. A crisis management plan should be developed to give clear guidelines to hospital staff to handle similar or more serious medication incidents.

CRISIS MANAGEMENT PLAN FOR MEDICATION INCIDENT IN AN ACUTE HOSPTIAL

The overall plan is illustrated in Figure 1. It comprises three phases: 1) preventive phase; 2) emergency phase in terms of assessment, implementation and follow-up; and 3) consolidation and reconstruction phase.

Preventive Phase

To be prepared is the key to successfully manage a crisis (Devlin, 2007), and several items should be addressed even before a crisis has arisen (Koster and Politis-Norton, 2004). One of the important steps is to identify potential crises. Recognition of potential crises enables management to plan for them and to enact measures to prevent the occurrence of such crises (Spillan, 2003). To prevent medication incidents, one should eliminate error, and identify errors early, before they reach the patients (Paparella, 2008b).

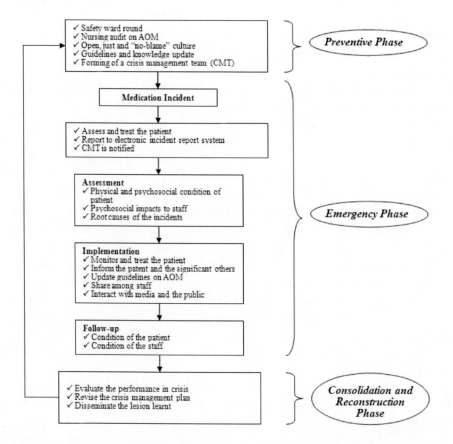

Figure 1. Overall Crisis Management Plan.

Routine safety ward rounds should be performed to survey the ward on medication safety. Current medication administration facilities, medication supply and storage of medication should be inspected to identify potential areas that will lead to medication errors. Flaws identified need to be fixed before they do any harm. A nursing audit on AOM should be done regularly to evaluate if nurses are familiar with and stick to the "5 Rights" rule and related guidelines. Wrong concepts and inappropriate practices should be corrected. This is even more important for newcomers to the ward (e.g. newly graduated staff) so as to ensure that they understand the ward's usual practices and their performance is up to standard.

In order to create sustainable medication safety changes, an open, just and "no-blame" culture should be maintained (Paparella, 2008a). This encourages constructive opinions from staff. Such a culture is also essential for maximum disclosure and review of medication errors (Emrich, 2010). Suggestions and reports from staff should be valued and carefully considered to improve the existing AOM system.

Guidelines on AOM and medication safety can also be revised according to the opinions collected and lessons learned from previous errors. These guidelines should be updated according to the advancing knowledge, and new knowledge should be shared among all staff.

A crisis management team (CMT) should be formed well before any crisis arrives. This is one of the golden rules in handling all sorts of crises (Koster and Politis-Norton, 2004). The CMT is responsible for planning for a crisis before it occurs (Spillan, 2003). It works together to achieve control of the crisis and minimize the impacts of the crisis (Devlin, 2007). It should consist of professionalss from multiple disciplines (Wiger and Harowski, 2003, as cited in Wong and Chan, 2009). A hospital administrator (e.g. hospital manager or chief nursing manager) is the team leader, and other members are representatives from frontline doctors and nurses, a patient safety officer, a public relations officer and a legal advisor.

Emergency Phase

Preventing harm to patients is the first priority during a crisis (Bacon, Morris, Runciman and Currie (2005). Once a medication error is discovered, the patient's condition is always the first thing to consider. The doctor in charge of the patient is informed to assess the patient at once, order investigations and prescribe treatments as needed. Nurses continue to monitor the patient's condition and provide treatments accordingly. If the staff involved is not at the scene (as in the case scenario), they should be informed to provide further information. When the patient's condition is stabilized, the nurse in charge of that shift reports the incident to the ward and department managers and also reports to the hospital through the electronic incident report system. After the patient safety officer receives the report, he/she calls for a meeting of the CMT to have an initial evaluation of the incident and lead the crisis management actions in the emergency phase, following the steps of assessment, implementation and follow-up.

Assessment

Continuous assessment is carried out for the patient (e.g. monitoring vital signs and performing blood and urine tests). The psychological aspects of the patient should also be addressed. This is because the medication incident is also a crisis for the patient, as it brings stress to the patient both physically and psychologically. Moreover, the psychological impacts to the staff involved need to be considered. They may have feelings of self-blame, loss of self-esteem and professional image, shame and culpability, and nurses may retain these emotional responses even years after medication incidents (Jones and Treiber, 2010).

Various aspects of the root causes of the error are investigated, including human factors, environmental factors, system factors, etc. As in the case scenario, the on-call doctor was not familiar with the medication preparation in the hospital, the nurses had inadequate competency in calculating the concentration and dose of the intravenous potassium chloride solution, the ward situation might have been too busy and distracted the nurses, and the nurses might have been too tired during night shift.

The CMT needs to assess the seriousness of the incident and estimate the level of interest and concern from media and public. The CMT also needs to consider the legal implication of the incident.

Implementation

Treatments and continuous monitoring are provided to the patient. The patient is referred to a professional for counseling (e.g. social worker, clinical psychologist) if there are indicated psychosocial needs. The patient and their significant others should be informed of what is happening. The doctor in charge of the patient, who is most familiar with the condition of the patient, should release the news accompanied by the nurse manager and a public relations officer. Besides giving the details of the medication incident and the following treatment plan, the doctor and the nurse should apologize and express regret and empathy to the patient. This can avoid a communication breakdown between healthcare professionals and the patient (Hoyle, 2005a).

Recommendations for existing practice and guidelines are made according to the analysis of the root causes of the incident. As in the case scenario, there is a need to update doctors about the medication preparation available in the hospital, and related information should be placed on the ward for quick reference. The communication and collaboration between doctors and nurses should be reinforced so as to prevent misunderstanding. Assessment and training on numeracy should be provided for nurses to reduce calculation error. The duty arrangement and workload of nurses also need to be reviewed to ensure that they are not over-stressed.

Debriefing is held among ward staff to share the incident, to tell them the facts, and to raise awareness about what has been learned since the incident happened. This is also a way to let the staff ventilate their feelings. Positive and encouraging messages are passed so as to affirm the working spirit. Counseling or professional referral is arranged for staff that have special psychological needs (especially for those directly involved in the incidents).

The CMT needs to be prepared to interact with the media. The spokesperson should have good communication skills and know the details of the incident. The speech should be carefully and well-structured so as to reduce social damage and preserve the confidence of the public in the hospital and healthcare system (Koster and Politis-Norton, 2004). A press release is issued to the media and public.

Follow-up

The patient has regular follow-ups with the doctor in charge and the counseling professionals to monitor their physical and psychosocial condition and to look for any long-term effects from the incident. Counseling follow-ups are also arranged for the staff with serious psychosocial stress from the incident.

Consolidation and Reconstruction Phase

The hospital's performance during the crisis is evaluated (Devlin, 2007). The crisis management plan is revised accordingly to make it more practical and effective. The lessons learned from the incident are disseminated within and between hospitals (Hoyle, 2005b).

IMPLICATIONS OF THE CRISIS MANAGEMENT PLAN

Medication incidents involve a diverse aspect of factors. It is impossible to completely eliminate medication incidents, no matter how perfect the prevention plan and guidelines are. When medication errors arise, it is always the frontline healthcare workers (doctors and nurses) who handle the situation in the first place. However, without a conscious management plan, they may not be able to deal with all the different problems effectively and efficiently. The suggested crisis management plan provides clear guidelines for them to follow, from the time when medication incident has not yet happened till it is over. They should understand the importance of this plan and be familiarized with it to ensure that they can act promptly and appropriately when crisis comes to them. Moreover, they should be well-equipped to handle crisis in the hospital. Studies revealed that medical and nursing graduates are often unprepared to deal with crisis in real work settings, and there are gaps in clinical training concerning aspects of clinical decision-making and the prevention, recognition and management of crisis (Flanagan et al., 2004). Thus, training workshops on crisis management for healthcare workers should be emphasized. The curriculum of the medical and nursing schools should also comprise basic crisis management to give an early insight of this issue to the students.

This crisis management plan is designed for the setting of an acute hospital. Medication incidents happen in convalescent hospitals, old-aged homes and other healthcare organizations, where administration of medication is required as well. This plan can be further adapted and developed to fit in diverse settings.

Medication incident is not the only patient safety crisis that hospitals are facing. Incidents like patient fall injury, wrong specimen labeling and wrong site surgery, also endanger the patients, the healthcare workers and the hospital. This crisis management plan can be a reference for developing specific plans for other incidents in the hospital.

CONCLUSION

Medication incident is one of the patient safety crises that is difficult to avoid. The hospital and all the healthcare workers should well prepare themselves to face this challenge. This paper demonstrates a detailed crisis management plan for dealing with medication incidents in acute hospital. The plan includes guidelines from the pre-crisis time to the post-crisis time, covering preventive, emergency and reconstruction interventions. It aims to lead the hospital through the crisis and minimize the damage done to patients, staff and the hospital. It is hoped that this crisis management plan can be adapted to different settings and other medical incidents. Doctors and nurses should be empowered with the knowledge and skills of crisis management so as to allow them to provide better care to patients.

AUTHOR'S BACKGROUND

Ms. Lam is a registered nurse in an acute hospital in Hong Kong. She has been working in the orthopedic and traumatology unit for seven years. She graduated from the Nethersole School of Nursing of the Chinese University of Hong Kong, and continues her studies in the Master of Science in Health Education program at the same university. (E-mail: teresalam@yahoo.com)

REFERENCES

Bacon, A. K., Morris, R. W., Runciman, W. B., and Currie, N. (2005). Crisis management during anaesthesia: Recovering from a crisis. *Quality and Safety in Health Care, 14*(e25). Retrieved 1 June, 2010, from http://qshc.bmj.com/content/14/3/e25.full

Bowen, K., Bitz, K., and Benner, P. (2010). Practice breakdown: Prevention. In P. E. Benner, K. Malloch, and V. Sheets eds. *Nursing pathways for patient safety*. St. Louis: Mosby.

Chan, T. Y. K. (2006). Prevention of medication error and unintentional drug poisoning in the elderly. *Hong Kong Medical Journal, 12*(5), 332-333.

Chan, Z. C. Y. (2009). Teaching crisis management in healthcare. In Zenobia C. Y. Chan ed. *Health issues in Chinese contexts Vol 1*. New York: Nova Science Publishers, Inc.

Devlin, E. S. (2007). *Crisis management planning and execution.* Boca Raton: Auerbach Publications.

Emanuel, V., and Pryce-Miller, M. (2009). Exploring the factors contributing to drug errors and how to improve knowledge. *Nursing Times, 105*(46), early online publication. Retrieved June 1, 2010 from http://www.nursingtimes.net/nursing-practice-clinical-research/clinical-subjects/patient-safety/exploring-the-factors-contributing-to-drug-errors-and-how-to-improve-knowledge/5008730.article

Emrich, L. (2010). Practice breakdown: Medication administration. In P. E. Benner, K. Malloch, and V. Sheets eds. *Nursing pathways for patient safety.* St. Louis: Mosby.

Farazmand, A. (2007). Learning from the Katrina Crisis: A global and international perspectives with implications for future crisis management. *Public Administrative Review, 67*(s1), 149-159.

Flanagan, B., Nestel, D., and Joseph, M. (2004). Making patient safety the focus: Crisis resource management in the undergraduate curriculum. *Medical Education, 38*, 56-66.

Fry, M. M., and Dacey, C. (2007). Factors contributing to incidents in medicine administration. *British Journal of Nursing, 16*(9), 56-59.

Hoff, L. A., Hallisey, B. J., and Hoff, M. *People in crisis: Clinical and diversity perspectives.* (6th ed.). New York: Routledge.

Hospital Authority. (2008). *Press release: HA relaunches medication reporting programme bulletin.* Retrieved June 1, 2010, from http://www.info.gov.hk/gia/general/200801/31/P200801310178.htm

Hospital Authority. (2009). *Risk Alert, 13.* Retrieved June 1, 2010, from http://www.ha.org.hk/haho/ho/psrm/HARA13th.pdf

Hospital Authority. (2010a). *Risk Alert, 16.* Retrieved June 1, 2010, from http://www.ha.org.hk/haho/ho/psrm/HARA16th.pdf

Hospital Authority. (2010b). *Press release: HA Convention 2010 – "Happy staff healthy people".* Retrieved June 1, 2010, from http://www.ha.org.hk/visitor//ha_visitor_index.asp??Parent_ID=10000&Content_ID=643&Dimension=100&Lang=ENG&Change_Page=2&Show_Archived=N

Hoyle, A. (2005a). A basic guide to patient safety. *British Medical Journal, 331*(7512), s55-a.

Hoyle, A. (2005b). A basic guide to patient safety (2): Risk analysis. *British Medical Journal, 331*(7516), s107.

Jones, J. H., and Treiber, L. (2010). When 5 rights go wrong. Medication errors from the nursing perspective. *Journal of Nursing Care Quality, 25*(3), 240-247.

Koster, M. C., and Politis-Norton, H. (2004). Crisis management strategies. *Drug Safety. 27*(8), 603-608.

Lalonde, C. (2007). The potential contribution of the field of organizational development to crisis management. *Journal of Contingencies and Crisis Management, 15*(2), 95-104.

Malloch, K., Benner, P., Sheets, V., Kenward, K., and Farrell, M. (2010). Overview: NCSBN practice breakdown initiative. In P. E. Benner, K. Malloch, and V. Sheets eds. *Nursing pathways for patient safety.* St. Louis: Mosby.

McConnell, A., and Drennan, L. (2006). Mission impossible? Planning and preparing for crisis. *Journal of Contingencies and Crisis Management, 14*(2), 59-70.

Nguyen, E. E., Connolly, P. M., and Wong, V. (2009). Medication safety initiative in reducing medication errors. *Journal of Nursing Care Quality, 25*(3), 240-230.

Paparella, S. (2008a). Choosing the right strategy for medication error prevention – Part II. *Journal of Emergency Nursing, 34*(3), 238-240.

Paparella, S. (2008b). Choosing the right strategy for medication error reduction – Part I. *Journal of Emergency Nursing, 34*(2), 145-146.

Parnell, J. A., Koseoglu, M. A., and Spillan, J. E. (2010). Crisis readiness in Turkey and the United States. *Journal of Contingencies and Crisis Management, 18*(2), 108-116.

Shane, R. (2009). Current status of administration of medicines. *American Journal of Health-System Pharmacy, 66*, S42-S48.

Spillan, J. E. (2003). An Exploratory model for evaluating crisis events and managers' concerns in non-profit organisations. *Journal of Contingencies and Crisis Management, 11*(4), 160-169.

Warburton, P. (2010). Numeracy and patient safety: The need for regular staff assessment. *Nursing Standard, 24*(27), 42-44.

Webster, C. S., and Anderson, D. J. (2002). A practical guide to the implementation of an effective incident reporting scheme to reduce medication error on the hospital ward. *International Journal of Nursing Practice, 8*, 176-183.

Wong, Y. Y., and Chan, Z. C. Y. (2009). Nursing crisis management: Fire safety in operating theatres. In Zenobia C. Y. Chan ed. *Health issues in Chinese contexts Vol. 2.* New York: Nova Science Publishers, Inc.

In: Crisis Management in Chinese Contexts   ISBN: 978-1-61761-609-9
Editor: Zenbobia C. Y. Chan   © 2011 Nova Science Publishers, Inc.

Chapter 6

CRISIS MANAGEMENT PLAN FOR HEALTH FOOD CRISIS AND RECALL PROCEDURES

S. Y. Leung[1] and Zenobia C. Y. Chan[2]
[1] The Chinese University of Hong Kong
[2] School of Nursing, The Hong Kong Polytechnic University

SUMMARY

Everyone likes to purchase safe and reliable food products. When the company or the government fails to assure the food-safety, it can be a crisis. Health food crises can have a crushing impact on the company, the government and the users. The coverage of product recall is large, from the manufacturer to the wholesaler, distributor or retailer. When a crisis hits, the company and the government are under a microscope. Whether you are a winner or loser all depends on how you handle and how well prepared you are for the crisis. However, Hong Kong's government was always retroactive on crisis and was always viewed as slow and messy when facing crisis. Preparing for a crisis is just as important as the response. Government and the concerned stakeholders should be looking at good crisis management strategies. A crisis management plan is prepared for sudden onset of health food crisis. The chapter serves as a reference for the related authorities to evaluate the current food safety policy. Otherwise, the company and the government would suffer losing the basic trust of the public and find their reputations seriously affected.

BACKGROUND

In 2008, the Hong Kong Health Food Association commissioned the University of Hong Kong Social Sciences Research Centre (Social Science Research Centre, 2008) to conduct research which indicated that about 35% respondents took health food. Health and food supplements compose a huge market locally. In recent years, the purchase of health supplements has become popular in Hong Kong due to a growing consciousness of personal health care among the public. There are product recall plans in the existing food recall system of the Centre for Food Safety. A crisis management plan specially designed for health food is absent. If health foods are "hazardous," it will become a huge crisis. Good risk management can improve the organization's ability to manage uncertainty, thus critical risks are detected before the problems come. The decision-maker is confident in their decision made through risk assessment and management (Curran, 2006). A comprehensive crisis management plan for health food is a must to define the responsibilities of the crisis management team and to provide the information necessary for different departments to handle a large-scale involvement. Quick and complete responses are the basic tenets in effective crisis management strategy (Daft & Dorothy, 2008). Through this sound crisis management plan, the food trade, consumer and government can be well prepared, minimize the risk, save lives and mitigate the negative impact of crisis (Runyan, 2006). We should work hand in hand to build Hong Kong into a world-class metropolis renowned for its food safety in facing health food crisis.

OBJECTIVE

The objectives of the crisis management plan are to:

1) identify the potential product hazards and key elements of an effective recall plan.
2) develop a holistic plan including notification activities, protocols, procedures, as well as a recovery plan in a health food crisis.
3) indicate an in-house coordinator and inter-departmental working team for the crisis management plan.
4) protect the welfare of public.

LITERATURE REVIEW

What is Health Food?

There is no global agreed definition for "health food" products. Different countries use different terms such as "dietary supplements," "nutraceuticals," "designed foods," "functional foods" and "natural health products" to refer to similar products.

The United States Congress has given a clear definition of "dietary supplement" in the Dietary Supplement Health and Education Act (DSHEA) (U.S. Food and Drug Administration, 2009) since 1994. A dietary supplement is a product taken by mouth that contains a dietary ingredient intended to supplement the diet. The dietary ingredients in these products may include: vitamins, minerals, herbs or other botanicals, amino acids, and substances such as enzymes, organ tissues, glandulars, and metabolites. Dietary supplements can also be extracts or concentrates, and may be found in many forms such as tablets, capsules, softgels, gelcaps, liquids, or powders. They can also be in other forms, such as a bar, but if they are, information on their label must not represent the product as a conventional food or the sole item of a meal or diet. Whatever their form may be, DSHEA places dietary supplements in a special category under the general umbrella of foods, not drugs, and requires that every supplement be labeled a dietary supplement.

In Europe, the definition of "food supplements" was clearly given in Directive 2002/46/EC of the European Parliament and of the Council on June 10, 2002. It refers to foodstuff with the purpose of supplementing the normal diet and which are concentrated sources of nutrients (i.e. vitamins or minerals, or other substances with a nutritional or physiological effect, alone or in combination), marketed in dose form(namely forms such as capsules, pastilles, tablets, pills and other similar forms, sachets of powder, ampoules of liquids, drop dispensing bottles, and other similar forms of liquids and powders), and designed to be taken in measured small unit quantities (EUR-Lex, 2002).

Hong Kong is lagging behind other developed nations in the area of health food products. There is no specific definition of health food in Hong Kong regulation. In the treaty of the "Plan of Action for Regulatory Cooperation on Natural Health Products" with Canada, natural heath products only include vitamins, minerals and traditional Chinese medicines (TCM). Non-traditional Chinese medicines, and herbal and health foods are not regulated. This is for sure the grey area in the Hong Kong food policy. The safety and the quality of health food is questionable under such incomplete and incompatible food policy.

LEGISLATION CONTROL OF HEALTH FOOD IN HONG KONG

There is no specific regulation of health food products in Hong Kong. The responsibility is unclear between the Department of Health and the Food and Environmental Hygiene Department. We apply the elimination method to distinguish which the health food products belong to which category, and who is the party ultimately responsible for it.

"health food" products that contain medicines are regarded as "pharmaceutical products" and "medicine." They are under the Pharmacy and Poisons Ordinance (Cap. 138) (Department of Justice, 2010a). The authority of these Ordinances lies with the Department of Health.

If the health food is comprised solely of "Chinese herbal medicine" and "proprietary Chinese medicine" as active ingredients and used for treatment and health promotion purposes, it is under the purview of the Chinese Medicine Ordinance (Cap. 549) (Department of Justice, 2010b). The authority of these ordinances lies with the Department of Health.

Health food products which cannot be classified as Chinese medicine or western medicine are regulated as general food products and are regulated under the Public Health and Municipal Services Ordinance (Cap. 132) (Department of Justice, 2010c), of which the Food and Environmental Hygiene Department is in charge.

There are "Guidance Notes on Classification of Products as Pharmaceutical Products" issued by the Department of Health, available at the website www.psdh.gov.hk (Department of Health, 2008). For Chinese medicines, the trade has to browse the website of the Chinese Medicine Council of Hong Kong at www.cmchk.org.hk.

It is the trade's responsibility to verify with the Department of Health, on their own, whether their health food products are classified as Chinese medicine, western medicine, or food.

Strictly speaking, Hong Kong has control of health food, but in such a loose and scattered way, that if a health food crisis comes, the result is imaginable.

What Crises Have Occurred Before?

A number of health food accidents have occurred in Hong Kong before. If health food has undeclared drug ingredients or another contamination or quality problem, it will seriously affect the user. In 2010, the Hong Kong government had 17 times called for a recall of a total of 52 problematic health food products. The following were just two, in a series of possible glitches, to show the ability of the Hong Kong government and the stakeholder to deal with health food crises.

The government did not discover a food safety problem in a health product commonly available to consumers in the market. until a woman complained to Department of Health of abnormal behaviour on December 20, 2009, after having consumed the slimming product for a period of time since July 2009. The women was discharged on February 8, 2010. The report of Government Laboratory showed the product had did not declare the western drug sibutramine, which would cause drug-induced psychosis and cancer-causing effects. The government finally called for the recall of the problematic health product, after a long delay of 3 months, on March 18, 2010 (Consumer Council, 2010).

Another faintly ridiculous incident of health food product recall was on May 5, 2010. Hong Kong authorities warned the public not to use a problematic batch of products after Singaporean authorities confirmed they were harmful. However, the same product was last passed in the Hong Kong surveillance program in 2009, and when the government called for recall, the local wholesaler told the pharmaceutical inspectors that they did not import such products. However, from the local list of registered proprietary Chinese medicines, a product with the same name and manufactured by the same mainland manufacturer was available here (Consumer Council, 2010b). The source and remains of the product was suspicious. Citizens were highly worried about whether food safety in Hong Kong was well under control by the Hong Kong government.

But the problem with health food products is really complicated. There were cases reported by the government every month, and that's just the tip of the iceberg. I must point out that further delay in crisis management would be unwise. Crisis management is definitely essential to protect citizens (Carole, 2007). A well-defined crisis management plan should be drawn up not only to solve the health food crisis that will inevitably occurr someday, but also to secure the public and the government.

Any Existing Plan?

There is a food recall plan currently running in Hong Kong (refer to Appendix I), but it is not designed for the complicated health food category. It's ridiculous to waste time exchanging words with other departments to clarify the department in charge of the problematic products when crisis comes.

However, there are still some loopholes in the current management policy. Firstly, the registration scheme for local traders is non-mandatory, and not all health food imported from other countries was distributed through local wholesalers. A small company with inconsistent operation schedules or production capacity can choose not to register in the scheme and sell on the market directly without any regular inspections and surveillance of government. Thus, the safety of health food is unknown. To attain a balance of food safety and a free market environment is a difficult task for government officials.

The Hong Kong government and its agencies cannot effectively and efficiently manage the outbreak of food crises. The overall charge of the outbreak is not clear. Based upon previous experience, coordinated and quick response cannot be made in case of large food recall which involves high political and media profile, and crosses geographical or organizational boundaries. It breaks both public health and public confidence. Also, the lines of authority between DH and FEHD are not clear during the outbreak. The relationships between the FEHD board, head office, advisory committees, hospital clusters, and hospital executives are not clear during the outbreak. DH and FEHD do not have the management structure and resources to deal with a major outbreak. The healthcare system is not flexible enough to respond to a major outbreak and most of the actions taken in the handling of a health food crisis outbreak are not backed up by legislation. The successful management of outbreak is dependent upon good and timely communication between relevant government departments and all stakeholders (Toigo, 2002). The relationship between the public/private hospitals and DH's regional offices should improve in any outbreak of food crisis.

Also, in line with the international trend, the Hong Kong government should incorporate more information and communication technologies to organize surveillance of information more efficiently and to perform more powerful and advanced analysis. The lesson learned from the health food recalls on May 5, 2010 and March 18, 2010 was that stakeholders should be involved to enhance the full use of the information system in health food crisis surveillance. Furthermore, advanced computerized system should be developed to generate early and reliable signals of outbreaks. Emergency preparedness and response can be undertaken at an earlier stage to protect communities, property and environment (WHO, 2007).

ACTION PLAN

A crisis management plan based on the risk-graded epidemiological scenarios to protect public is suggested. This plan will be activated when there is a report of an unpermitted or undeclared substance, or a quality problem in a health food product. It is depicted in two possible scenarios.

The first scenario is to check and stop the problematic health food before import to Hong Kong.

The second scenario is the faulty health food product has been imported into Hong Kong and is selling on the retail level. There is enough evidence to prove it contains an unpermitted/undeclared substance or quality problem with the product that will seriously affect the public.

In addition to the existing measures, the following preparedness measures are adopted before the crisis.

An effective crisis management plan should be detailed with appropriate information such as important telephone numbers, media contacts, media response sheets, spokesperson information, containment procedures, evaluation forms, emergency telephone numbers, crisis control center information (Saravara, 2007).

RECALL CONTACT LIST (PRE-CRISIS)

No matter what the scenario is, an updated database should be developed to record all the initial information of each health food in detail. We could ferret out the product in our management system at once when crisis comes. We need to intensify our work to make our system information-based. Importer information, such as name, address, telephone number, and amount of product imported, is needed.

Product details, such as product name, package type and size, identifying codes/ lot number, quantity of the batch, ingredients and photo of products, manufacturer contact name, telephone and fax numbers, date of production, and quantity to be in distribution channels, are required.

Wholesaler or retailer details, such as distributor list of wholesalers and retailers, names and addresses of stores and distribution information, are needed.

First of all, an impact assessment should be conducted by the crisis management team for the preparation of the problem. The report will provide a detailed overview of the situation. Stakeholders can focus on key issues with different levels of recall priority set out in the crisis management plan. The timeliness of the assessment is critical and it should be completed within 24 hours.

The details of the problems should be record clearly, including the date and time of the report, the nature of the problem, test results and other investigation reports.

Other relevant information is type of hazard, assessment of risk to user, proposed action, and chemical/ biological analysis report.

According to Courtright & Smudde (2010), suggested recall priority is set depending on the seriousness of the problem.

1) Serious level (Emergency crisis situation)
2) Health food contains an undeclared ingredient or quality failure so that the use of the product will cause death directly or serious health problem
3) High level
4) Health food contains an undeclared ingredient or quality failure which may cause an adverse health effect.
5) Low level
6) Health food contains an undeclared ingredient or quality failure not likely to cause adverse health effect.

First Scenario –Check and Stop the Problematic Health Food Before Import to Hong Kong

According to the recall contact list, the problematic health food can be stopped before it is imported to Hong Kong. The Food and Environmental Hygiene Department (FEHD) and Customs and Excise Department (CED) are responsible for stoping the importation before release to the market.

Second Scenario – The Food Has Been Imported into Hong Kong, Selling on Retail Level. There is Evidence Confirmation of Undeclared or Non-Permitted Substance Or Quality Failure that Will Seriously Affect the Public

A procedure adopted to meet an emergency of product recall is illustrated as follows. A health food product contains an undeclared drug ingredient and use of the product has caused several deaths directly. The health food is popular and used by all age groups. The food must be removed from the market quickly.

ASSEMBLE THE RECALL MANAGEMENT TEAM

The chairperson of recall team is the director of the Food and Health Bureau. DH and FEHD are partners in the management of food crisis. As the public health authority, DH concentrates on the management of victims while FEHD is responsible for food products recall. As the health food may fall within the food or drug categories, the recall management team should contain different specialists in medicine, Chinese Medicine, and nutrition. The name of the person in the individual department should be obtained and also a replacement individual for when the person is not available.

The Recall Committee should involve a group of members that receive the initial information from different channels. They are responsible for the implementation of action and communication.

The Recall Assessors Team includes a group of public health physicians, a nutritionist, biotechnologist, food scientist, and other specialists in food, microbiology, toxins and chemicals, Chinese medicine practitioners and doctors to investigate the health food problems and make the recommendation to recall or not.

1. Identify All Products to be Recalled

When based on the information provided by the recall assessors team, the product recall committee makes the decision to proceed with the product recall, the chairperson will initiate the following actions: inform different affected stakeholders, develop a recall plan, activate the recall management team to execute the function, obtain details about illness and patients', and arrange for investigator to take samples of specific analysis to Government Laboratory for confirmation.

Public Health Issue

DH conduct an epidemiological / clinical investigation to determine the cases, the source of hazards is identified by the Centre for Health Protection. Government Laboratory also provides laboratory support for testing and diagnosis of substance.

Hospital Authority (HA) is responsible for the surveillance of patients who have relevant symptoms. Risk assessment on patients is conducted. The utility rate of hospital is assessed.

2. Implementation of the Recall Plan

Information Services Department (ISD) makes an announcement to the staff in the Food and Health Bureau (FHB). The contact details of the person in charge should be included in the announcement. Daily updates to internal staff are made through the intranet, SMS and e-mail. A hotline for centralized information enquiry is established.

The recall is in a state of emergency. According to Altman (2005), information typically protected can be released in an emergency to protect public health. The recall committee should release the product information to the media at the first instance. A coordinator is responsible for necessary follow-up actions and channeling all necessary communications. He should have the list of ingredients in the health food and which ingredient is hazardous. He should inform importers, distributors, and retailers of the affected product details for identification of the products by e-mail, facsimiles and letter. The reason for the health food recall and hazard involved are explained to them in the correspondence. Clear instruction on how to handle the product is given to them.

Public warnings are given through mass media announcements including radio, TV, newspapers, the internet, and a press release. Contact numbers for general enquiry, importers, distributors, and retailers are provided. Daily status reports are also provided to the public.

The raw ingredients in the hazardous health food are traced. Verification of the raw ingredients of the finished products needs to be recalled by chemical/ biological analysis. The team members should collect data on the location of products involved and subject to recall. It is also required to obtain the amount of the product sold.

In monitoring the recall plan, all data available are reviewed and it is decided whether further data is required. Quality check of recalled products is done daily to monitor the progress.

Verification of investigations by telephone calls and site visits ensures all importers, wholesalers and retailers have taken appropriate action and measures the effectiveness of the plan.

Recall committees provide complete documentation and weekly progress reports to the chairperson until the closure of recall process. The information should include the quantity of products recalled and estimated time frames for the remainder of completion of recall.

FEHD assists the Environmental Protection Department (EPD) by organizing proper disposal of the products after recall. The Government Logistic Department (GLD) provides the logistics support.

A final report is prepared by the recall committee on the recall procedures. The report should involve the following information: reason of recall, details of recall plan, recalled product records, and method of destruction.

In order to facilitate the recall procedures, a recall plan was suggested to the private company. if the following measures are adopted before the crisis, there are a lot of measures in relation to food recall can moderate.

Recall procedures suggested for company (Food Safety Authority of Ireland, 2008)

1) The owner/CEO should coordinate the entire recall plan.
2) The distribution section should stop all distribution of questionable materials and arrange for return of product to collection points. They should also prepare an inventory and distribution status of the product showing where, when, the quantity of, and to whom the product was shipped.
3) The production and quality assurance section should prepare batch identification, halt production of product if related to the problem, investigate the cause of the problem and check all records.
4) The consumer affairs section should prepare a response for consumers and answer all consumer enquiries.
5) The accounting department should set up a stock reconciliation system to determine the cost of recall.
6) The legal counsel section should handle legal implications.

7) The public relations department should handle press releases in all media.

8) The technical department should obtain batch identification and samples, obtain product analysis to determine if pick-up or destruction is necessary, and consult with regulatory agencies if a recall is required.

9) The marketing section should notify sales managers and brokers, arrange for pick-up at retail levels and arrange for proper credit to be given.

10) Regional sales managers should aid in contacting customers and assist in product pick-up and delivery of credit notes.

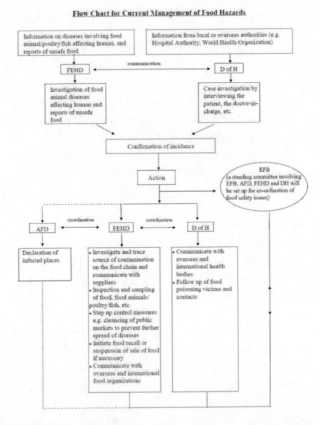

Figure 1. Flow Chart for Current Management of Food Hazards. From *"Information on diseases involving food animal/poultry/fish affecting human, and reports of unsafe food,"* by Food and Environmental Hygiene Department, 2005.

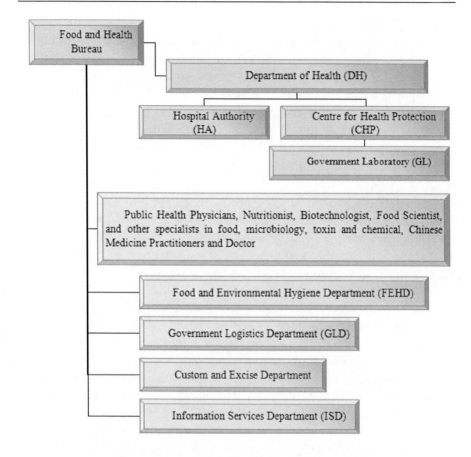

Figure 2. Command Structure for Health Food Recall during Serious Level.

DISCUSSION

Prevention, preparation and containment are three cardinal stages in crisis management (Daft & Dorothy, 2008). Through crisis management, we can know how the organizations handle the events (Runyan, 2006). However, the current food safety policy of Hong Kong is not up to the challenges caused by technological, economic and socio-cultural changes in the food system. It does not consider the sense of consumer's protection and many grey areas in the legislation increase difficulty in enforcement.

The status of Hong Kong is very special as it was a British colony and has now been returned to Mainland China. There is a large variety of food from different countries with different standards being imported into Hong Kong. Different countries have different food safety management systems, and this may lead to confusion between quality and safety, over regulation, selective enforcement, lack of integration of food laws in the overall legislative system, the multiplicity of responsible agencies, and the mismatch between the required standards. So, we should seek harmonization in the world trade by simplifying the laws, and help in formulating management systems in most of the countries (Okezie, 2005).

In Hong Kong, a comprehensive, mandatory registration scheme for food importers and distributors of health food should be established. Under the scheme, importers and distributors would be required to maintain proper transaction records of imported health food, so that in the event of a food incident, the sources and points of sale of the food concerned could be traced by the government swiftly and thoroughly. Under the new legislation, when public health is under serious threat, the authorities would be empowered to require all wholesalers and retailers to stop selling and recall the food concerned.

Different measures are used in different sections by the government in dealing with food crisis. The government should attain the same standard among the entire monitoring system. A sustainable education program to train people's behaviour in crisis management is needed (Blum et al., 2004).

Moreover, the government should step up efforts in the sampling and testing of health products being sold on the market, as well as in updating the law. It should also liaise closely with relevant experts and academics as well as consumers. Through listening to their views on food safety standards, the government can ensure that our people can eat with peace of mind and our policy can attain international standards with other countries and meet the changing needs.

CONCLUSION

Strategically, health food regulated through control at the source, sample testing at import, wholesale and retail levels and a border monitoring system will offer local health food an extremely high level of protection in terms of its hygiene and safety.

We should never sell ourselves short, but we should also not set a task for ourselves which is utterly ridiculous. A crisis management plan for health food crisis is designed. However, there may still be some room for refinement. This is just a stimulus for the government and the trade. They need to investigate this topic further.

AUTHOR'S BACKGROUND

The first author holds a master's degree in health education granted by the Chinese University of Hong Kong, and has been working as a health inspector in a local food and health authority for 12 years.

REFERENCES

Altman, S. (2005). Legal aspects of crisis-management communication: What to communicate. *Athletic Therapy Today*, 6 –10.

Blum, R. H., Raemer D. B., Carroll J. S., Sunder, N., Felstein D. M., Cooper J. B. (2004). Crisis resource management training for an anaesthesia faculty: a new approach/h to continuing education. *Journal of Medical Education, 38*(1), 45-55.

Consumer Council, (2010a). *Public urged not to consume products with undeclared ingredients.* Retrieved May 31, 2010, from http://www. consumer.org.hk/website/ws_en/consumer_alerts/recalls_and_alerts/2010 031801.html

Consumer Council. (2010b). *Mainland Chinese medicinal product found to have exceeded Singapore's lead limit.* Retrieved May 31, 2010, from http://www.consumer.org.hk/website/ws_en/consumer_alerts/recalls_and_ alerts/2010050502.html

Courtright, J. L., Smudde, L. J. (2010). Recall Communications: Discourse Genres, Symbolic Charging, a-nd Message Design. *International Journal of Strategic Communication, 4*(1), 58-74.

Curran, K. M. (2006). Value-Based Risk Management (VBRM). *Cost Engineering, 48*(2), 15-22.

Daft R. L. & Dorothy M. (2008). *Understanding Management (Sixth ed.).* Cengage Learning, 200, USA.

Department of Health. (2008). Guidance Notes on Classification of Products as "Pharmaceutical Products" under the Pharmacy and Poisons Ordinance (Cap. 138) http://www.psdh.gov.hk/eps/eng/html/Guide_on_PRClass.pdf

Department of Justice. (2010a). *Pharmacy and Poisons Ordinance (Cap. 138).* Retrieved May 21, 2010, from http://www.legislation.gov.hk/blis_pdf.nsf /6799165D2FEE3FA94825755E0033E532/0F66D4839C78DBDA482575 EE00438DD5/$FILE/CAP_138_e_b5.pdf

Department of Justice. (2010b). Chinese Medicine Ordinance (Cap. 549). Retrieved May 21, 2010, from http://www.legislation.gov.hk/blis_pdf.nsf /6799165D2FEE3FA94825755E0033E532/31AD50AD264E25A6482575 EF00197027/$FILE/CAP_549C_e_b5.pdf

Department of Justice. (2010c). *Public Health and Municipal Services Ordinance (Cap. 132).* Retrieved May 21, 2010, from http://ww w.legislation.gov.hk/blis_pdf.nsf/6799165D2FEE3FA94825755E0033E53 2/40DC34E06542CFE1482575EE003FE971/$FILE/CAP_132_e_b5.pdf

EUR-Lex (2002). Directive 2002/46/EC of the European Parliament and of the Council of 10 June 2002 on the approximation of the laws of the Member States relating to food supplements. Retrieved May 24, 2010, from http://eur-lex.europa.eu/LexUriServ/LexUriServ.do?uri=CELEX:32002L0046:EN: NOT

Food Safety Authority of Ireland. (2008). *Guidance Note No. 10: Product Recall and Traceability (Revision 1).* Retrieved May 26, 2010, from http://www.fsai.ie/WorkArea/DownloadAsset.aspx?id=736

Lalonde, C. (2007). The potential contribution of the field of organizational development to crisis management. *Journal of Contingencies and Crisis Management, 15*(2), 95-104.

Okezie, I. A. (2005). The impact of food regulation on the food supply chain. *Toxicology, 221* (1), 119-127.

Runyan, R. C. (2006). Small business in the face of crisis: identifying barriers to recovery from natural disaster. *Journal of Contingencies and Crisis Management, 14*(1), 12-26.

Saravara, S. (2007). Business Continuity Planning in Higher Education Due to Pandemic Outbreaks. *Journal of Security Education, 2*(3), 41-51.

Social Science Research Centre. (2008). *HK Public Knowledge of Health Supplements.* Hong Kong University. October 22.

Tura, N. D., Reilly S. M., Narasimhan S. & Yin, Z. J. (2004). "Disaster Recovery Preparedness Through Continuous Process Optimization", *Bell Labs Technical Journal, 9*(2), 147-162.

U.S. Food and Drug Administration. (2009). *Overview of Dietary Supplements.* Retrieved May 31, 2010, from http://www.fda.go v/Food/DietarySupplements/ConsumerInformation/ucm110417.htm#what

World Health Organization (2007). *Mass casualty management systems: strategies and guidelines for building health sector capacity.* Switzerland: WHO Document Production Services.

APPENDIX

Import Control and Food Safety Guidelines

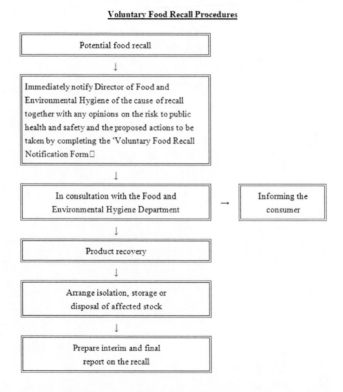

Voluntary Food Recall Procedures

Potential food recall

↓

Immediately notify Director of Food and Environmental Hygiene of the cause of recall together with any opinions on the risk to public health and safety and the proposed actions to be taken by completing the 'Voluntary Food Recall Notification Form'

↓

In consultation with the Food and Environmental Hygiene Department → Informing the consumer

↓

Product recovery

↓

Arrange isolation, storage or disposal of affected stock

↓

Prepare interim and final report on the recall

Figure 3. Voluntary Food Recall Procedures. From Food and Environmental Hygiene Department. Retrieved May 31, 2010 from http://www.cfs.gov.hk/english/import/import_icfsg_08_chart.html

In: Crisis Management in Chinese Contexts   ISBN: 978-1-61761-609-9
Editor: Zenbobia C. Y. Chan   © 2011 Nova Science Publishers, Inc.

Chapter 7

SCHOOL CRISIS MANAGEMENT PLAN FOR ADOLESCENT DRUG ABUSERS

W. F. Chau and Zenobia C. Y. Chan
School of Nursing, The Hong Kong Polytechnic University

SUMMARY

The prevalence rate of adolescent drug abuse arises dramatically. Many school drug abuse incidents were reported. The crisis of student drug abuse is different from other crises. Society is highly sensitive to and aware of the incidents of adolescent drug abuse. The roles and duties of the crisis management team and the crisis management plan are discussed to help schools to mitigate the impact of student drug abuse. The risk factors and protective factors of adolescent drug abuse are highlighted. The ways for schools to proactively protect the students from taking illicit drugs are also discussed. It is hoped that the crisis management framework of this chapter can provide a good foundation for schools to respond to school drug abuse incidents effectively and promptly.

INTRODUCTION

Crises, disasters, emergencies and catastrophes can be defined by a rigid set of criteria or individual perceptions. Nevertheless, crises are characterized by severe and largely unexpected threats, high uncertainty and the need for urgency in decision making (McConnell and Drennan, 2006).

School is an institution designed for students to learn safely under the supervision of teachers. However, any of the crises, such as fires, explosions, earthquakes, floods and also suicides, grief, loss, school shootings, gang activity, sexual and physical abuse, medical emergencies, deaths caused by drug addiction, or kidnappings and human trafficking, can unexpectedly occur in schools and have great impact on school settings. Such crises lead to public panic, unsafety and, most importantly, disruption of routine functioning of the educational process (Mariana-Viorica and Cătălina-Ioana, 2009; Allen et al, 2002). The routine functions of school should be resumed as soon as possible with the intervention of crisis management.

"Crisis" is defined as "a time of decision" in Webster's New Collegiate Dictionary and "crisis management" is defined as "special measures taken to solve problems caused by a crisis" (Devlin, 2007, p.1-4). When a crisis happens, the school should prevent it from spreading and limit its duration. As no school is immune to crisis, the establishment of a school crisis management team to formulate different crisis management plans becomes mandatory for the education authorities. This is because the early recognition of a potential crisis can lead to an effective action and prevent, or at least diminish, the impact caused (Cornell and Sheras, 1998).

Plenty of the guidelines for formation of school crisis management team are rendered by education authorities in various countries. However, most of the guidelines are dealing with the crises involving alcohol-related fatality, self-injurious behavior, school suicide, racial conflict and community violence (Cornell and Sheras, 1998). Illicit drug use becomes an acute global problem after surveying the websites of several international narcotics control organizations (Shek, 2007). As Hong Kong is an international city and under the influence of popular culture, which can be reflected by the incidents of young singers from Hong Kong being arrested in Japan for possessing drugs, adolescent substance abuse is a grave concern (Lam, 2010). Moreover, there is a lack of research on school crisis management for adolescent drug abuse in the context of Hong Kong.

ADOLESCENT DRUG ABUSE IN HONG KONG

Although a high-level interdepartmental task force on youth drug abuse was formed by the Chief Executive of the Hong Kong Special Administrative

Region, P.R.C. in 2007 and the Secretary for Justice was appointed to lead the task force to combat adolescent drug abuse from a holistic perspective such as preventive education and publicity, treatment and rehabilitation, law enforcement, research and external co-operation (Shek, 2007), the number of reported cases of adolescent drug abuse did not mitigate. The strategies used for tackling the problem by the government do not understand the problem from an ecological perspective.

A study was conducted by The Hong Kong Polytechnic University (PolyU) and the Christian Zheng Sheng College in the spring and summer months of 2009, with a view toward further understanding drug abuse on school campuses, by collecting data from 443 participants recruited from three counseling centers for psychotropic substances abusers and nine residential drug treatment centers. The study showed that there were 129 schools with students abusing drugs on the campus, including 109 secondary schools, four primary schools and four special schools; nearly half of the respondents had abused drugs on school campus. It also indicated that there were 53 schools with students selling drugs on school campus, including 50 secondary schools, one primary school and two special schools. Sixty-six respondents (14.9%) had sold illicit drugs in their schools. It also revealed that there were 52 schools with students buying drugs on school campus, including 49 secondary schools, two primary schools and one special school. Seventy-two respondents (16.3%) bought illicit drugs in their schools. It also found that ketamine, ecstasy, cannabis and "pills" were popular drugs consumed, sold and bought by students on campus (Chan, 2010 April).

Likewise, the quantity of ketamine found within the first seven months of 2009 was twenty times more than that of the same period the previous year. The huge supply of smuggled ketamine exacerbates the vulnerable young people's easy access to drugs and develops a youth sub-culture of drug abuse (Lam, 2010). Hence, the incidents of drug abuse occurring in schools are not rare. The incidence of drug abuse may sink schools into a crisis. The community is highly sensitive to the incidence of school drug abuse and shows solicitude for the issue. The impact of drug abuse incidence on school image is devastating.

CRISIS MANAGEMENT

Crisis management planning is not a science; it is more of an art. It is because science is the operation of general laws as obtained and tested through scientific methods, but art is the skill acquired by experience, study or observation (Devlin, 2007). Framework and guiding principles are useful for formulating a crisis management plan. However, crisis is different each time and every school is unique (Education Bureau, 2005). School personnel may fail to recognize problem situations and leave them unaddressed which can precipitate crisis events or worsen an existing crisis. Prompt response that leads to an effective action and prevents or, at least, reduces the impact of crisis is necessary for schools (Cornell and Sheras, 1998). An effective crisis management team can facilitate a school to act quickly and responsibly in a crisis (Education Bureau, 2005). A successful crisis management can turn "a crisis" into "an opportunity" which may affect the survival of schools nowadays.

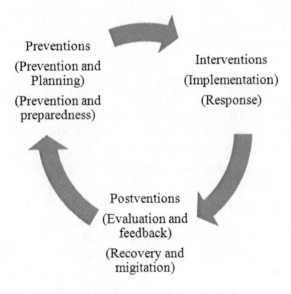

Preventions
(Prevention and Planning)
(Prevention and preparedness)

Interventions
(Implementation)
(Response)

Postventions
(Evaluation and feedback)
(Recovery and migitation)

Figure 1. The stages of Crisis Management Planning.

The crisis management involves preventions (pre-crisis stage), interventions (acute-crisis stage) and postventions (post-crisis stage) (Education Bureau, 2005; Devlin, 2007). The preventions are prevention programs, support services, crisis intervention teams, and emergency plans and drills. The interventions activate the school crisis plan, emergency procedures, notification, communication, debriefing and short-term crisis counseling. The postventions are referrals for long-term counseling or other services, and evaluation of the intervention and programs (Knox and Roberts 2005).

Prevention and planning, implementation, and evaluation are the three main stages in managing crisis (Ritchie, 2004). The crisis management can also be more comprehensively involved in five phases: Prevention, Preparedness, Response, Recovery and Mitigation (Regional Office of Education). Figure 1 shows the stages of crisis management planning.

Figure 2. The five essential elements of effective crisis management in schools.

The five essential elements of effective crisis management in schools are shown in Figure 2 (Montana Office of Public Instruction, 1999).

1) The Policy and Leadership: It provides both a foundation and a framework for action. The chances of effectively managing a crisis are increased with a community level plan and individual building plans, which are tailored to the conditions and resources of the individual school. Leadership is necessary to ensure an effective implementation of plans and maintenance of preparedness.
2) The Crisis Management Team: A school crisis management team can be a highly effective organizational unit for dealing with a variety of crises.

3) The School Crisis Management Plan: The plan should be written, updated as often as necessary, and given to every staff member. The plan should identify clearly what response is needed in each emergency situation so that staff members will know in advance how to react in times of crisis.

4) Communications: When a crisis occurs, effective communication is essential--within the school, with parents and the community, and with the news media, which is often the fastest conduit to the public. Effective communication can speed the restoration of equilibrium; conversely, poor communication can make a bad situation much worse.

5) Training and Maintenance: Preparation for and response to crises rely on people's understanding of the policies and procedures and knowing what they are to do. These are achieved through training. Maintaining preparedness is an ongoing process that involves debriefing following crises, periodic review and updating, and ongoing training.

THE SCHOOL CRISIS MANAGEMENT TEAM

Schools must respond to a drug-related incident in a way that is authoritative, consistent and fair (Department of Education and Training, 2006). The goals of school crisis management team are safety (to ensure the immediate safety of all students, teachers and staff), stability (to have a quick recovery of school routine), consistency (to control the flow of information so as to eliminate the spread of rumor), prevention of further injury (to identify at-risk students for necessary intervention, to protect the privacy of involved students and to be aware of secondary reactions), support of individuals and groups (to provide effective counseling and to mitigate post-incident delayed reactions) and empowerment of students' response capabilities (to enhance the students' personal growth through effective coping with the crisis situation) (Education Bureau, 2005).

The functions of the school crisis management team are drawing up a school crisis management plan, collecting and clarifying ongoing information about the crisis, evaluating the impact of the crisis on the school, coordinating all resources (in and outside school), responding quickly to crisis, providing support to teachers, students and parents, coordinating the progress of the crisis management, evaluating the crisis plan and coordinating the follow up work (Johnson, 2000). To achieve the above functions, the leader should be competent not only in good management but also strong leadership.

There is no way a single principal or vice-principal can manage the many aspects associated with a crisis. Principals must rely on other key school personnel to perform tasks, but the number of personnel involved should be limited so that the privacy of related students can be protected. The suggested roles of the crisis management team are team leader, teacher liaison member, parent liaison member, community liaison member, school social worker, educational psychologist and other members such as teaching assistants (Education Bureau, 2005). In order to protect the privacy of the students involved, some roles can be assigned to some personnel. The suggested roles and personnel of school crisis management team are shown in Figure 3 below (The Hong Kong Federation of youth groups, 2010).

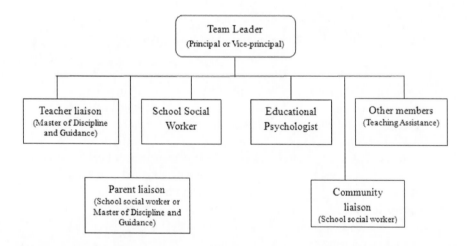

Figure 3. The organizational structure of school crisis management team.

The members of the team must have the trust of the students and teachers, have the ability to remain calm in tense situations, have the authority to make decisions, have the knowledge and skills to be a helpful resource and be perceptive of and sensitive to the feelings of others (Education Bureau, 2005).

Conoley, Hindmand, Jacobs, and Gagnon (1997) identify ten common mistakes made by school leaders. There is a tendency among some leaders to function in a reactive mode, ignoring potential problems until it is too late. To be successful, school leaders must have a well-developed vision of their schools. In addition to vision, school leaders must be able to communicate their ideas effectively, set clear and reasonable expectations for others, and maintain a sense of common purpose and collaboration among school staff (Duke, 1987). That is why the leader is the spirit of the team.

THE ROLES AND DUTIES OF CRISIS MANAGEMENT TEAM

For a crisis team to function effectively, at a minimum the members must share common goals, have well-defined roles and duties and be willing to work together in a coordinated manner (Cornell and Sheras, 1998). The roles and duties of each member of the crisis management team are listed in the tables below (The Hong Kong Federation of youth groups, 2010; Education Bureau, 2005; Policy Statement 2-C17, 2010; Thompson and Rosemary, 1990):

Team Leader—Principal or Vice-principal

Roles:	Duties:
• Formulates the crisis management plan • Assesses the situation • Makes the important decisions • Gives the directions to others • Supervises and coordinate the events of crisis management	a. Verifies the source of information b. Keeps the principal informed about the actions taken if the leader is not school principal c. Notifies school management board, school supervisor and the regional education officer and seeks help if needed d. Calls an urgent crisis management team meeting and activates the crisis management procedure e. Announces the crisis events to students f. Renders the support to teachers through teacher liaison member g. Renders the support to parents through parents liaison member h. Prepares for media enquires i. Reviews the crisis management plan and plans follow-up actions j. Conducts an evaluation of the effectiveness of the crisis management

Teacher Liaison Member—Master of Discipline and Guidance

Roles:	Duties:
• Coordinates the support for teachers and staff in handling the crisis	a. Keeps a phone tree and record forms and facilitates their use when necessary b. Arranges and assists school principal in conducting staff debriefing meeting c. Updates the crisis information for teachers d. Prepares and distributes the material for special class periods e. Arranges substitute teachers for teachers who have difficulties conducting special class periods f. Pays attention to the progress of special class periods and provides assistance as needed

Parent Liaison Member—School Social Worker or Master of Discipline and Guidance

Roles:	Duties:
• Coordinates support for the victim's family • Coordinates the communication with parents	a. Contacts the victim's family and provides the support b. Contacts the parents of all affected students c. Prepares and distributes the circular for parents d. Arranges the reply for parent inquiries e. Arranges parent conferences if necessary

Community Liaison Member—School Social Worker

Roles:	Duties:
• Coordinates with community resources to provide support to school, teachers and students	a. Keeps a community resource list b. Liaises with outside agencies for support and their referral procedures c. Consults with teacher liaison member, parent liaison member, school social worker and educational psychologist about the needs of seeking community support services

School Social Worker or Discipline and Guidance Teacher

Roles:	Duties:
• Supports the school by providing counseling to students, teachers and parents	a. Provides support to the victims and their family b. Identifies other helpful resources for students and teachers, and also the referral services c. Conducts individual or group meetings with students or teachers as needed d. Helps screen students at risk e. Assists teachers in conducting special class periods

Educational Psychologist

Roles:	Duties:
• Provides professional advice and support	a. Assists school in managing the psychological impact of the crisis and developing a crisis management plan b. Provides immediate emotional support for teachers c. Provides individual or group debriefing to students and teachers in need d. Prepares and assists teachers conducting special class periods

Other Members—Teaching Assistants

Roles:	Duties:
• Assists other team members to smoothen the crisis management when necessary	a. Designates rooms for different uses and make this known to all staff b. Is familiar with all procedures and their relevant information and forms c. Assists in preparing and delivering the material for special class periods d. Assists teachers conducting special class periods

The supports and assistance provided from community partnerships such as the school-police liaison officer, social worker of narcotic agencies and regional education officer are essential in dealing with student drug abuse incidents. The school-police liaison officer can provide some professional legal advice regarding drug abuse, educating students about the harmful effect of drugs and the criminal offense of drug trafficking.

PROCEDURES FOR MANAGING A DRUG RELATED INCIDENT

Some schools practice suspension or expulsion for drug abusers. Many cases show that expulsion can reflect a failure to take proactive or preventive action in drug abuse (Conoley *etal*, 1997). Schools should engage the students involved in an education or training pathway as the priority. Students involved may be placed at further risk if they are out of school for an extended period. Stigmatizing students and alienating them from the school community may compound the marginalization, and social, economic and health problems faced by the most at-risk young people. The consequences of being caught with drugs at school should not cause more harm than the drug use itself (Department of Education and Training, 2006). Schools should cultivate a safe and supportive environment for students instead of scaring and blaming students.

Schools can manage any school drug abuse incident as the following flowchart suggests in Figure 4 (Department of Education and Training, 2006; The Hong Kong Federation of youth groups, 2010).

Prevention is better than cure. Drug use is a complex social issue that must be addressed by the cooperative actions of the whole community. Schools and parents have an important role in the prevention of drug use and in early intervention for students who may be at risk of developing drug use problems (Department of Education and Training, 2006). An effective action plan and strategies to tackle the adolescent drug abuse problem should be formulated according to the risk factors and the protective factors (Shek, 2007). It is more cost effective to allocate more resources in the prevention phase of crisis management than in the intervention phase.

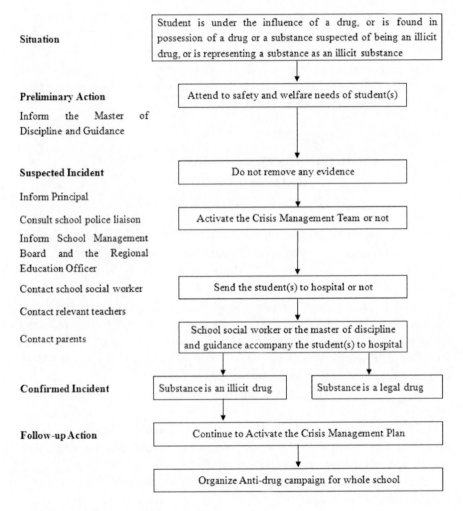

Figure 4. The Flowchart for handling school drug abuse incidents.

PROTECTIVE FACTORS TO FIGHT AGAINST ADOLESCENT DRUG ABUSE

The ecological perspective identifying the risk and protective factors of adolescent drug abuse is usually employed to formulate intervention strategies (Shek, 2006). There are numerous studies showing that various risk factors at the individual level (meaninglessness), family level (growing up in nonintact families), school level (low academic achievement) and community level (growing up in deprived communities) increase the chance of drug abuse in adolescents (Weissberg et al, 1991; Felner and Felner, 1989). Smith and Carlson (Smith and Carlson, 1997) suggested that optimism (individual level), parental support and guidance (family level), and supportive nonparent adults (community level) are protective factors for adolescents facing ecological hazards.

The study conducted by Hong Kong PolyU and the Christian Zheng Sheng College mentioned above indicated that over half of respondents felt that they did not get enough correct drug knowledge from the formal curriculum, and over half of respondents felt that they did not get enough life skills education from the formal curriculum. It unveils the failure of schools focusing on the academic achievement of students but neglecting the developmental needs of the students.

School is the battlefront for protecting adolescents from abusing drugs. Schools should foster a harmonious and caring culture and environment so that they become a community of love, care and trust. A set of positive and healthy values and virtues should be developed. Schools should implement a clear healthy school and drug-free policy for all. The knowledge of dangerous drugs, their harmful effects and the prevention of drug abuse should be incorporated into the curriculum. Anti-drug educational activities such as small group discussions, talks and seminars should be organized regularly (The Catholic Diocese of Hong Kong, 2009). Schools should implement more preventive measures, as suggested above, to diminish the drug abuse incidents from occurring.

CONCLUSION

The occurrence of drug abuse incidents may happen in any school. The impact of drug abuse on schools is enormous, which may lead to the survival of school in Hong Kong context nowadays. An effective crisis management team with frequent tabletop exercise can not only mitigate the effect on the school, but also protect the privacy of students involved. The formation of a crisis management team with clearly defined roles and duties and the procedures of handling drug related incident are discussed. It is worthy for schools to use it as reference. Since many risk factors of drug abuse are related to family, the crisis management for adolescent drug abuse in families can be discussed in future.

ABOUT THE AUTHOR

Mr. Chau Wang Fai is a registered secondary teacher in Hong Kong. He graduated with a Bachelor of Science (Biology) in 1994 from Hong Kong University of Science and Technology. He has been teaching science and biology in secondary school for fifteen years. Mr. Chau is the Master of Social Service and a member of the School Administrative Committee. He is teaching the subject of Health Management and Social Care of New Senior Secondary curriculum which was implemented in 2009. Therefore, he is enriching his knowledge by working towards a master's degree in health education at The Chinese University of Hong Kong.

REFERENCES

C Mariana-Viorica, B Cătălina-Ioana (2009). Involvement and action - school preparation program for crisis situations. *International Conference on Economics and Administration*, 113-118

Chan SC (2010, April) PolyU and Zheng Sheng College jointly present survey findings. Media Releases.

Conoley, J.C., Hindmand, R., Jacobs, Y., and Gagnon, W.A. (1997). How schools promote violence. *Family Futures*, 1, 8-11

Department of Education and Training (2006). Drugs in Schools, Guidelines for Managing Drug Related Incidents in Schools. Australia: New South Wales Government.

Dewey G. Cornell , Peter L. Sheras (1998). Common errors in school crisis response: Learning from our mistakes. *Psychology in the Schools*, 35(3), 297-307.

Duke, D. (1987). School leadership and instructional improvement. New York: Random House.

Education Bureau (2005). School Crisis management. Hong Kong: Education Bureau.

Edward S. Devlin (2007). Crisis management planning and execution. Auerbach Publication.

Fairfax County Public Schools. Crisis Management Workbook. Virginia: Fairfax Country Public Schools.

Felner R.D., and Felner T.Y. (1989) Primary prevention programs in the educational context: a transactional-ecological framework and analysis. In

Primary Prevention and Promotion in the Schools. Bond, L.A. and Compas, B.E., Eds. Sage, Newbury, CA. pp 13-49

Johnson, K. (2000). School crisis management-- A hands-on guide to training crisis response teams. Hunter House Publishers.

Knox, K.S. and Roberts A.R (2005) Crisis Intervention and Crisis Team Models in Schools. *Children & Schools*, 27(2), 93-100

Lalonde, C. (2004). In search of archetypes in crisis management. *Journal of Contingencies and Crisis Management, 12*(2), 76-88.

Lam R (2010) Beat Drugs on School Campus. House of Tomorrow, 18(1), 1-6

M Allen, K Burt, E Bryan, D Carter, R Orsi, L Durkan (2002). School Counselors' Preparation for the Participation in Crisis Intervention. *Professional School Counseling*, 6(2), 96-102

McConnell, A., & Drennan, L. (2006). Mission impossible? Planning and preparing for crisis. *Journal of Contingencies and Crisis Management, 14*(2), 59-70.

Montana Office of Public Instruction (1999). Safe Schools and Crisis Management Guidelines, Strategies and Tools. Helena: Safe and Drug-Free Schools and Communities.

Policy Statement 2-C17 (2010). Crisis Management Planning in Catholic Schools. Australia: Catholic Education Commission of Western Australia.

Ritchie B.W. (2004). Chaos, crises and disasters: a strategic approach to crisis management in the tourism industry.

Shek, D.T.L. (2006) Conceptual framework underlying the development of a positive youth development program in Hong Kong. *Int. J. Asolesc. Med. Health*, 18, 303-314.

Shek, D.T.L. (2007) Tackling Adolescent Substance Abuse in Hong Kong: Where We Should and Should Not Go. *TheScientificWorldJOURNAL*, 7, 2021-2030.

Smith C. and Carlson B.E. (1997) Stress, coping and resilience in children and youth. *Soc. Serv. Rev.* 71(2), 231-256.

The Catholic Diocese of Hong Kong (2009). Stand on Drug Prevention in Catholic Schools. Hong Kong: The Catholic Diocese of Hong Kong.

The Hong Kong Federation of Youth Groups (2010). New Healthy School Anti-Narcotis Resource Kit (Book 3) Hong Kong:The Hong Kong Federation of Youth Groups.

Thompson, Rosemary (1990). Suicide and Sudden Loss: Crisis Management in the Schools. ERIC Clearinghouse on Couseling and Personnel Services Ann Arbor MI. ED315700

Weissberg R.P., Caplan M., and Harwood R.L. (1991) Promoting competent young people in competence-enhancing environments: a systems-based perspective on primary prevention. *J. Consult. Clin. Psychol.* 59, 830-841.

In: Crisis Management in Chinese Contexts   ISBN: 978-1-61761-609-9
Editor: Zenbobia C. Y. Chan   © 2011 Nova Science Publishers, Inc.

Chapter 8

A Crisis Management Plan about Medical Errors: Oxygen Errors

Mandy S. M. Chan[1] and Zenobia C. Y. Chan[2]

The Chinese University of Hong Kong[2] School of Nursing, The Hong Kong Polytechnic University

Summary

With the flooding of reports of medical errors by the media everyday, the public is now more concerned about the issue of patient safety. Health care sectors have been putting great effort into preventing these occurrences. Numerous reports of different medical errors have been investigated, however, oxygen therapy, a commonly used medical treatment, is rarely mentioned. It can pose a risk to the patient and lead to serious consequences if not handled well.

This paper provides evidence of how medical errors related to oxygen therapy can harm patients, illustrates a crisis management plan using the prevention, emergency and consolidation phases framework to manage medical incidents related to oxygen errors, and provides some implications for public health and health care professionals.

Introduction

Crisis exists in our everyday life: it happens to affect our personal life, the business of the companies surrounding us, and even the country we live in.

Health care is one of the most crisis-prone industries in the world. The incident rate of medical errors in the U.S. can be as high as to contribute to the eight leading causes of death, and many of these errors are preventable (Miller, 2003). Good crisis management of medical errors is a crucial step toward maintaining and promoting patient safety.

This paper consists of three objectives: first, to have an overview of medical errors related to oxygen therapy worldwide; second, to discuss a crisis management plan related to the issue concerned; and third, to discuss its implications to public health and health care professionals.

LITERATURE REVIEW

Crisis and Crisis Management

A crisis is a change, which may be sudden or which takes some time to evolve, that results in an urgent problem with a high level of uncertainty that must be addressed immediately (Efficiency Unit, 2009, P.4). A diversity of crisis exists in our daily life. They can be personal matters, like being diagnosed with an acute disease; organization issues, like financial difficulties due to defective product; or global affairs, such as the volcano eruption in Iceland that caused chaos in travel in Europe (Sing Tao Daily, 2010). Crisis is often viewed as a danger because it may negatively affect the reputation, image and income of an individual or organizations, however, Devlin (2007) believes crisis also means opportunity. He states that a good crisis manager not can not only minimize the danger of a crisis to an organization, but can also seek to maximize every possible opportunity through good crisis management. At the acute phase of crisis, the situation may be so chaotic that the executive and the members of an organization can make wrong decisions. Therefore, a crisis management plan--a plan detailing the actions that the executives want to be taken during crisis--can help the organization to get ahead of the situation, practice procedures that limit the damage to the organization or victims, and prepare background information for instant release to media or stakeholders. The crisis management team will be responsible for developing this plan and will take charge during crisis in order to manage the crisis in a prompt and effective manner.

Crisis and Crisis Management in Health Care Sector

Health care, nowadays, is facing many different crises. The health care expenditure is ever increasing due to the increased burden of disease of the aging population worldwide, unhealthy lifestyles of people, and the advance of technology in medical treatment. The public expects high quality, low cost health care services, and this always creates tension between the health care sector and the general public concerning the financial issue.

Infectious disease pandemics are another crisis of concern. With the globalization of the world, infectious disease is no longer an isolated issue within a region or country. The Severe acute respiratory syndrome (SARS) outbreak provided us with a disastrous example of how infectious diseases can affect the health of people in the whole world, and cause a disaster to the whole health care system, leading to a discontinuation of health care services, damage public health, and cause loss of life of health care professionals (Buus, and Olsson, 2006; Tseng, Chen and Chou, 2008). Furthermore, patient safety is also identified as another challenging crisis. Patients who are admitted for medical treatments with the intention of restoring their health, are then suffering unnecessary harm due to medical errors. Reports of medical errors, such as wrong diagnosis of a patient with breast cancer due to misidentification of a patient's specimen (Ming Pao, 2008) and wrong route of drug injection leading to a fatal event of a 21-years old lady (Headline Daily, 2007) that occurred in Hong Kong, have greatly damaged the image and credibility of the local health care sectors. If the medical errors get into the court, a huge amount of compensation fees will be expected. In fact, medical error is not a new event to be researched and reported throughout the last 20 years (Mewshaw, White, and Walrath, 2006). They state that as many of 98,000 patients may die from preventable medical errors in a given year, and an analogy is made about the frequency of medical errors being equivalent to one jumbo jet crashing each day. Lau (2002) thinks that a health care system that has not put patient safety as a high priority will contribute to the problem. Patient safety should never only rely on a particular individual to prevent errors; but it requires the health care organizations to achieve the objective to create a safety culture. It includes all the organizational structures and processes, working place and equipment, the qualification standards of the staff, and their relationships that shape them in a way that enable safe behaviors to be carried out (St. Pierre, Hofinger, and Buerschaper, 2008).

Medical Errors Related to Oxygen Use and Handling

The enormity of medical errors has been studied. Among those incidents, medication errors, wrong operation site and retaining of medical equipment in patients' bodies are often reported. Many guidelines and risk reduction programs are designed to solve these incidents. However, the author finds that medical incidents related to oxygen use and handling are rarely reported and studied. Oxygen is administered to a patient for a variety of purposes in chronic and acute cases as a medical treatment because it is essential for a person's metabolism and normal physiological functions. Discontinuation of oxygen therapy in critical patients can be fatal. According to the National Patient Safety Agency, the UK received 281 incident reports related to inappropriate administration and management of oxygen between December 2001 and June 2009 (National Patient Safety Agency, 2009). Some of the incidents are related to wrongly administering other medical gases, rather than oxygen, due to confusion of the two gas flow meters (Waite and Maccartney, 2003) or failure to deliver oxygen due to poor quality of design of the gas cylinder (Adekanye and Wali, 2003). In fact, problems related to oxygen incidents compromise patient safety the most during patient transport (Pesanka et al., 2009). The author also experienced, more than once, that patients who required oxygen therapy were transported with an empty tank. Fortunately, early detection of the problem and reconnection of oxygen sources to patients prevent further harm. Medical errors which did not lead to severe events are not being reported. For instance, Brokalaki et al.'s (2008) study to look for the antibiotic and oxygen omissions and errors in hospitalized patients found that oxygen errors occurring in the study group are as high as 27.4% in two hospitals in Greece related to its prescription, administration and compliance of patients. This study used a prospective approach. Researchers collected data by direct visits to the patients and review of their medical records reflected more of the extent of oxygen errors. The problem of oxygen errors may be onlythe tip of iceberg, as many errors that did not lead to severe harm were underreported. An example of oxygen error occurring in Hong Kong will be illustrated as a case scenario for the discussion of how a crisis management plan can deal with the problem.

Case Scenario

A terminally ill patient was scheduled to have a follow-up in an outpatient clinic. During the consultation, the patient expressed symptom of shortness of breath and the pulse oximetry showed that she had a saturation level below

90%. It was found that she had malignant pleural effusion after the doctor reviewed her chest X-ray. Therefore, the doctor ordered 4 L/min via nasal cannula to be administered to her and she needed to be admitted to ward for further treatment. The patient then received oxygen therapy through the wall outlet in the clinic. While waiting to be admitted, her saturation level returned to normal after receiving oxygen. After receiving the admission call from the ward, a nurse and two supporting staff assisted the patient transfer from a bed to a stretcher. One of the supporting staff prepared the oxygen cylinder, connected the nasal cannula and administered 4L/min oxygen to her. It was observed that the oxygen regulator meter pointer was in the green zone (ON). The patient was then transported to the ward by a porter. Her relatives accompanied her for the whole process. Upon arrival at the ward, the patient was found cyanotic and experienced respiratory arrest. Another supporting staff of the ward discovered that there was no oxygen outflow from the gas cylinder when the oxygen supply was reconnected to the wall outlet. It was discovered that the cylinder valve knob was not turned on. The nurses in the ward immediately initiated assessment of the patient's vital signs, prepared the crash cart, called the house-officer and case medical officer and performed cardiopulmonary resuscitation as the patient deteriorated in her condition. The relatives were shocked by the sudden change in the patient's condition; they started to cry and lost emotional control. The nurse in charge was informed of the situation and she invited the relatives to wait outside during resuscitation. Then, she informed the ward managers (WM) of the ward and the outpatient clinic, and the department operation manager (DOM) to investigate and take charge of the incident. Unfortunately, the patient was certified after an hour of resuscitation. The incident was reported to the hospital through the Advanced Incidents Report System after initial understanding of the events of that day.

After the incident, the department and the hospital involved certainly faced a critical crisis; inappropriate handling will lead to serious consequences. In this case, a comprehensive and well-planned crisis management plan would have definitely helped the nurses, departments and hospitals to cope with the situation and prepare for further occurrence of medical errors.

Crisis Management Plan Related to Medical Errors

The plan for crisis management related to medical errors is illustrated below. It utilizes the framework of three phases during crisis: prevention, emergency, and consolidation and reconstruction. Each phase will further discussed in detail in macroscopic (health care system/ hospital) and microscopic level (department/individual).

PREVENTION PHASE

This phase includes the concept of mitigation and planning (Runyan, 2006). Crisis management teams in the health care system are required to plan for sentinel events related to medical errors, determine preventive measures for their occurrence, and the actions they need to do during crisis.

At the macroscopic level, Hospital Authority (HA), a statutory institution responsible for managing the public hospital in which the medical errors occurred, has a well-developed policy and system to manage sentinel events occurring in public hospitals. Under the system of HA, quality and risk management is the unit responsible for promoting patient safety and managing medical errors. It is considered as the crisis management team at the hospital level. As stated by Tzeng (2005), use of terms "crisis management" and "risk management system" is interchangeable in medical disputes, as they should all be both institutionally based and strategic, consisting of policies, procedures, planning and actions toward prevention of medical disputes. HA introduced a sentinel event policy in 2007 to further strengthen the reporting, managing and monitoring of serious medical incidents (Hospital Authority, 2009). Under the 3R concept in risk management (risk data, risk reduction program, and risk circle), HA has implemented various actions to deal with medical incidents. Risk data are collected and analyzed through reports in the Advance Incidents Report System (AIRS), complaints and safety ward rounds. The data will then be used to develop risk reduction programs, for example, medication safety, Time-Out procedure for identifying correct site and procedure, and preventing patient suicide. Risk circle is maintained through the learning and sharing of data and programs in meetings, forums and publications to health care professionals. The quality and risk management team also ensures the quality of health care services by facilitating the development of protocols and standards at the hospital level, performing regular audits of clinical skills and performance (Lui, 2008). However, in this case scenario, there is a lack of risk data related to oxygen incidents and the author has not seen any risk reduction program or audits related to temporary oxygen It is suggested that crisis management should identify the related risk of oxygen therapy and implement relevant risk reduction programs and actions to deal with the problem.

At the development level, strategies implemented to reduce oxygen errors included placing notice cards at the bedside of patients receiving oxygen therapy, monitoring their oxygen saturation in routine assessments, regular checks of the oxygen cylinder's function and the replacement of empty tanks everyday by supporting staff. Informal training (through verbal instruction or demonstration) has been provided to new staff about the use of oxygen by senior nurses or colleagues of the supporting staff only. Obviously, in this case scenario, the supporting staff was unaware that cylinder valve knob was not turned on as the meter pointer was in the green zone(ON). The non-compliance with the practice of the oxygen cylinder operation of the staff probably led to the event. When the author reviewed the medical gas operation manual in HA, it was found that the manual was a 2002 version and only the English version was available. Supporting staff may not be able to read the manual. Therefore, at the department level, common procedures and standards or manuals should be translated into a written Chinese version in order to enable the supporting staff have access to it and formal training should be provided for them. Furthermore, checking the availability of oxygen before patient transport by a nurse may have prevented the event.

EMERGENCY PHASE

The emergency phase starts from the point that crisis has occurred. It is extremely important because it is point in time thata crisis management decision can save lives or lessen the damage of the crisis (Runyan, 2006). Devlin (2007) has identified four steps that need to be carried out by the crisis management team: take charge of the crisis quickly, gather information about the crisis and establish the facts, tell the story to appropriate groups, and take actions to fix the problem.

In this case scenario, nurses in the department, including WM, DOM, nurse in charge, and the medical officers in the ward served as a crisis management team in the emergency phase. They took charge to manage the crisis once the patient was admitted. There are three parties that are of concern: the victim, the victim's relatives and the supporting staff involved. The first immediate actions should be implemented for the victim. Assessment of the patient's vital signs, informing the medical officer and preparing the crash cart for further emergency medical treatment are the prompt actions needed to reverse the problem. If the victim survivves, continuous monitoring of her condition and the extent of harm should be evaluated. Nurse managers and the senior medical officer should gather information about the crisis at this time. They should understand the whole process that led to the event by questioning the supporting staff, the nurse and the porter responsible for patient transport, and establish the facts by interviewing their staff and investigating the oxygen cylinder that was used for any defects or problems. As for the involved staff, managers should support them with reassurance. Blaming the staff members will not help in the crisis, because they are already suffer enough from the emotional stress and worries after the occurrence of the incident. Staff will demand more support during crisis (Tzeng and Yin, 2008), so the crisis leader should put themselves in the position of the involved staff and recognize their needs (Devitt and Borodzicz, 2008) in order to maintain the trust between management and employees, which is identified as a key factor in good crisis management (Tseng, Chan and Chou, 2005). Lau (2002) also echoed this with the view that a "non-punitive" environment is the first step to make a hospital a high reliability organization.

Victims and/or their relatives are the most challenging parties to deal with in cases of medical error. If they are not handled well, the incidents may immediately become the headline of the next day's newspapers, and the hospital may face lawsuits and need to pay a big sum for compensation due to the errors. If as in this case, the relatives are emotionally unstable during the event, the nurse in charge can provide an isolated room for them to calm down and cope with their emotion. The event should be disclosed to the relatives of the victim. HA has provided its employees with guidelines for the management of sentinel events, or seriously untoward events, pertaining to the interview with victims/their relatives. It suggests that the victim and victim's relatives should be interviewed by a department head or another senior, and experienced, staff in order to acknowledge an unanticipated outcome has occurred and they should be informed that the health care team are making every effort to ensure the patient receives the best possible management. They should also be reassured that the event will be investigated and someone will keep in contat with them to update them with information after the initial meeting (So, 2010). In this case scenario, when the relatives were first informed of the incident, some were very angry and shocked and expressed that they might pursue a lawsuit. They were in the stage of grief for their loved one; a crisis leader should be able to understand their feelings and show empathy to them. At the second interview, the relatives decided to abandon action after receiving a sincere apology from the department and hospital, because they considered the fact that the patient already had terminal cancer and a cure was not possible.

At the macroscopic level, the crisis management team needs to communicate with the department heads once the department informs them of the situation. An investigation team/ root cause analysis team should be formed within the first 48 hours of sentinel events and untoward events to gather information and investigate the cause within two weeks. At the same time, the human relations and chief executive of the hospital should prepare a press release or be prepared to be questioned by the media. Legal advice from lawyers should also be obtained if the victims pursue a lawsuit. Once the emergency phase is under control, the consolidation and reconstruction phase begins.

CONSOLIDATION AND RECONSTRUCTION PHASE

This is the phase in which an organization seeks to minimize the impact of the crisis and learn from the event (Runyan, 2006). This can be lengthy and sometimes endless depending on the type of crisis (Devlin, 2007).

At the hospital level, the crisis management team should continue to gather information and investigate using the root cause analysis. It is a process of asking what, how and why the event happened and what should be done to prevent it. Instead of blaming individual human errors, it also looks into the factors of organizational processes and structures by which errors are not prevented (Mengis and Nicolini, 2010). They should hold regular meetings in order to update the process of the investigation and submit a final report to hospital chief executive and headquarter of Hospital Authority. Then they should gather what has been learned in the event and make possible change to prevent further episodes. In this episode, the crisis management team recommended three improvement actions (Hospital Authority, 2010). The first action is to promote good practice of oxygen administration to all clinical staff by sharing the event in Risk Alert publication. As suggested by the author before, the operation manuals for medical gas handling should be updated and also translated into a Chinese version in order to meet the needs of some of the clinical staff. The National Patient Safety Agency (2009) also echoed the view that a multidisciplinary team should be established to review oxygen-related incidents and develop a local oxygen policy and training program. The second action is to ensure nursing staff performs a final check of all medical devices before patient transfer. Nurses, who are responsible for supervising the supporting staff, should bear the responsibility of ensuring patient safety. The author suggested the adoption of the "Ticket to Ride" project done in hospitals in the U.S. It is a literal "ticket" to accompany patients from the ward unit to the procedural unit. It includes a pre-transport assessment and checklist, as well as relevant patient information, in order to facilitate the handoff communication between two units and increase awareness of the patient's condition and medical equipments before transport. It was also proved to be effective in reducing off-unit oxygen-related events (Pesanka et al., 2009). The third action recommended is to liaise with the Hong Kong Oxygen Company for improvement of the open/close indicator for all oxygen cylinders. This change of the equipment structure would definitely minimize the confusion in identifying whether the value knob of oxygen cylinder is turned on or not.

At the department level, the nurse manager should identify other risks that may lead to oxygen incidents in the ward and outpatient clinic. They should also perform oxygen handling related assessment among other staff members and provide appropriate training. The nurse manager in this department reviews the safety manuals about medical gas and shares with her staff members important points to note in a debriefing meeting. Follow-up actions and referrals should be implemented for the involved staff and the victims. The emotion and working ability of the supporting staff should be assessed, and staff should be referred to a staff crisis support team if necessary. A change of working position can be considered if the staff cannot cope with the incident. As the victim died eventually in this event, follow-up actions would be done with victim's relatives only. Arrangement of clinical psychology services can be provided to help them deal with the trauma and the process of bereavement.

IMPLICATION FOR PUBLIC HEALTH AND HEALTH CARE PROFESSIONALS

People seek health care services for restoration of or to maintain their health status. The occurrence of medical errors can harm public health by causing unnecessary suffering, complications, and even death. Therefore, to enhancing patient safety through the use of the crisis management approach would be appropriate to manage and reduce the harm related to medical errors done to both the patients and health care organizations.

This discussion paper highlighted the knowledge gap between patient safety and oxygen errors and called for prompt action to review and investigate the crises related to oxygen. The author illustrated that oxygen errors are less frequently reported than other errors. This does not mean they rarely occur; instead, health care professionals are less aware of the potential hazard unless it develops into serious event. A crisis management plan focusing on the prevention phase should be emphasized before the crisis occurs again. The author suggested a review of oxygen incidents, an update of policy, and training related to oxygen administration and handling should be carried out to protect public health from unintentional medical errors.

Crisis management is highly emphasized in many other disciplines in order to guide their actions in various crises. In health care settings, it is also rooted in the contingency planning for disaster, infectious disease outbreak and the policy for sentinel events. Not only health care professionals at the managerial level should be equipped with knowledge about crisis management; frontline staff should also be provided with the training. By providing them with comprehensive training in crisis management, they can understand the process of crisis and apply crisis management strategies not only to serious events at the hospital level, but also in their daily work. They can also give suggestions to the hospital crisis management team about different contingency plans or implement the plan in a less chaotic manner during crisis.

Conclusion

This paper discusses crisis management related to medical errors. An overview of literature about crisis management and medical errors has been provided. A case scenario is presented to illustrate how a crisis management plan can guide health care organizations and health care professionals in dealing with the crisis. Finally, it concludes by providing the implications for health care professionals in promoting patient safety. The author hopes that further research can be carried out by applying this crisis management approach to manage medical errors.

Author's Background

Mandy is a registered nurse in Hong Kong. She holds a bachelor's degree in nursing (honors) from The Chinese University of Hong Kong and has been working in a public hospital for five years. She is furthering her master's studies related to health education and promotion in the Chinese University of Hong Kong, and hopes to strengthen her professional knowledge about promoting health in her clients and in the general public.

REFERENCES

Adekanye, O., and Wali, A. R. (2003). Oxygen delivery failure. *Anaesthesia,* *58*, 90-191.

Brokalaki, H., Matziou, V., Brokalaki, E., Merkouris, A., Fildissis, G., and Myriantbefs, P. (2008). Antibiotics and O2 omissions and errors in hospitalized patients. *Journal of Nursing care Quality*, *23*(1), 86-91.

Buus, S., and Olsson, E. K. (2006). The SARS crisis: Was anybody responsible? *Journal of Contingency and Crisis Management, 14*(2), 71-81.

Devitt, R. K., and Borodzicz, E. P. (2008). Interwoven leadership: the missing link in multi-Agency major incident response. *Journal of Contingencies and Crisis Management, 16*(4), 208-216.

Devlin, E. S. (2007). *Crisis management planning and execution.* Boca Raton: Auerbach Publications.

Efficency Unit. (2009). *Crisis Management-An international Overview.* Hong Kong : Efficency Unit. Retrieved June 4. 2010 from http://www.e u.gov.hk/sc_chi/publication/pub_bp/files/crisis_management.pdf

Headline Daily.(2007). Retrieved June 4,2010 from http://www.hkheadline .com/news/instant_news_content/200707/07/20070707a134444.asp

Hospital Authority. (2009). *Annual Report on Sentinel Event*: 1 October 2007-30 September 2008. Hong Kong: Hospital Authority.

Hospital Authority. (2010). *Risk Alert.* Hong Kong: Hospital Authority. Retrieved May 20, 2010 from http://www.ha.org.hk/h aho/ho/psrm/HARA15th.pdf

Lau, D. H. (2002). Improving patient safety and reduce medical errors. *Hong Kong Medical Journal*, 8(1), 65-67.

Lui, S. F. (2008). *Quality Management in hospital practice. Current movement and issues of Quality and Risk Management in Hospital Authority.* Retrieved 28 May, 2010 from http://www.hkcem.com/html/training /files/Quality%20Management% 20in%20Hospital%20Practice.pdf

Mengis, J., and Nicolini, D. (2010). Root cause analysis in clinical adverse events. *Nursing Management, 16*(9), 16-20.

Mewshaw, M. R., White, K. M., and & Walrath, Jo. (2006) Medical errors: Where are we now? *Nursing Management*, 37(10), 50-54.

Miller, S. R. (2003). *Medical Errors Prevention*. Florida: Health Care Institutions. Retrieved May 20,2010 from http://www.affectplus .com/MedErrors.pdf

Ming Pao. (2008). Retrieved June 4,2010 from http://hk.news.yahoo.com/ article/080919/4/8b01.html

National Patient Safety Agency. (2009). *Rapid Response Report: Oxygen Safety in hospitals*. UK: National Patient Safety Agency. Retrieved May 28,2010 from

http://www.nrls.npsa.nhs.uk/resources/type/alerts/?entryid45=62811

Pesanka, D. A., Greenhouse, P. K., Rack, L. L., Delucia, G. A., Perret, R. W., Scholle, C. C., Johnson, M. S., and Janov, C. L. (2009). Ticket to ride: Reducing handoff risk during hospital patient transport. *Journal of Nursing Care Quality*, *24*(2), 109-115.

Runyan, R. C. (2006). Small business in the face of crisis: identifying barriers to recovery from a natural disaster. *Journal of Contingencies and Crisis Management, 14*(1), 12-26.

So, H. Y. (2010). *Procedures for Management Events and Serious Untoward Event*. Hong Kong: Hospital Authority New Territories East Cluster Cluster Committee On Quality and Risk Management.

St. Pierre, M., Hofinger, G., and Buerschaper, C. (2008). *Crisis Management in acute care settings: Human factors and team psychology in a high stakes environment*. Berlin: Springer.

Tseng, H. C., Chen, T. F., and Chou, S. M. (2008). SARS: Key factors in crisis management. *Journal of Nursing Research, 13*(1), 58-65.

Tzeng, H. M. (2005). Crisis management policies and programs to prevent nursing-related medical disputes in Taiwanese hospitals. *Nursing Economics, 23*(5), 239-247.

Tzeng, H. M., and Yin, C. Y. (2008). Crisis management systems: staff demand more support from their supervisiors. *Applied Nursing Research, 21*, 131-138.

Sing Tao daily. (2010) Retrieved June 4, 2010 from http://hk.news.yah oo.com/article/

100509/3/hwhn.html

Waite, A., and Macartney, I. (2003). Air-oxygen flowmeter confusion. *Anaesthesia, 58*, 194.

In: Crisis Management in Chinese Contexts   ISBN: 978-1-61761-609-9
Editor: Zenobia C. Y. Chan   © 2011 Nova Science Publishers, Inc.

Chapter 9

CRISIS MANAGEMENT PLAN FOR HANDLING TEACHER SUICIDE

Y. Lee and Zenobia C. Y. Chan
School of Nursing, The Hong Kong Polytechnic University

SUMMARY

There have been numerous cases of teacher suicide in the past decade. Most of the tragedies are related to mental disorders and huge work-related pressure. The tragedy of teacher suicide causes a negative impact on students, colleagues and the school. There must be a long period of time to compensate for the loss. Therefore, a crisis management plan for handling teacher suicide for schools is need. The objective of the plan is to assist teachers suspected of being at risk for suicide and to equip school staff with appropriate knowledge and skills to facilitate a quick, coordinated and direct response in the event of a teacher suicide. The crisis management framework consists of three phases (the pre-crisis phase, the acute-crisis phase and the post-crisis phase). The plan is beneficial to all schools in preventing, handling and following up the tragedy of teacher suicide.

INTRODUCTION

A psychological crisis occurs when a stressful life event overwhelms an individual's ability to cope effectively in the face of a perceived challenge or threat. (Mitchell, Everly, 1989, p.103)

A psychological crisis maybe thought of as a response condition wherein:

1) psychological homeostasis has been disrupted;
2) one's usual coping mechanisms have failed to reestablish homeostasis; and
3) the distress engendered by the crisis has yielded some evidence of functional impairment. (Mitchell, Everly, 1989, p.103)

Suicidal behavior is a major global public health problem. Hong Kong's suicide rate has increased gradually (The Hong Kong Jockey Club Centre for Suicide Research and Prevention, view on 25th May, 2010). Among the tragedies in the education sector, there have been numerous teachers suicide cases related to their workload pressure from year to year. The extra non-teaching workload, non-school working hours and uncertainties of education reform causes over 50% of teachers to suffer from tension, muscle pain and physical fatigue, which are signs and symptoms of the stress arousal phase (Hong Kong Professional Teachers' Union, 2005, p.6). It has been reaching an alarming stage at whicht teachers suffer from intolerable work-related stress, which if not managed well will become mental illness and develop symptoms of suicide (Suicide Prevention Services, 25th May, 2010).

There are lots of helplines, workshops and campaigns on suicide crisis management for students in Hong Kong. There were lots of resources for different sectors in assisting students suspected of being at risk for suicide. But there is seldom any resource to teach one to recognize a teacher's emotional problems, and there is no channel for people to seek help if a teachers attempts to kill himself / herself.

We cannot wait until another school teacher plunges to death. It is our loss if one more respectable frontline teacher who feels helpless and hopeless commits suicide. Therefore, a crisis management plan for teacher suicide should be introduced aimed at raising public awareness of the pressure faced by teachers, to assist teachers suspected of being at risk for suicide, and to design a plan to equip school staff with appropriate knowledge and skill to facilitate a quick, coordinated and direct response to a teacher suicide incident.

LITERATURE REVIEW

Crisis Management

"Crisis management" (CM) could be defined as "special measures" taken to solve problems caused by a crisis. (Devlin, 2007, p.1) Crisis management planning (CMP) is not science that covers general truth or the operation of general laws, as obtained and tested through scientific methods. Instead, it is more of an art with skills acquired by experience, study or observation. (Devlin, 2007,p.2) The crisis management plan is a documented plan detailing the actions the executives need to take when a crisis strikes the organization. It is designed to put order to confusion. After a crisis has surfaced, the executives who have been selected to serve on the crisis management team (CMT) will work together to achieve control of the crisis in order to minimize the impact of the crisis (Devlin, 2007, p.2).

Overview of Suicide in Hong Kong

Based on the statistical data from the Hong Kong Jockey Club Centre for Suicide Research and Prevention and Coroner's Court, the suicide rate has risen steadily over the past 30 years. Middle-aged people have become a high-risk group. More males committed suicide than females. Females in Hong Kong have a higher suicide rate than that of global. Jumping from a height is the most common method of suicide and is of particular concern (HKJC Centre for Suicide Research and Prevention, 25th May, 2010)

Research points out that 80% of the suicidal people will have signs and symptoms before committing suicide. These include cognitive, emotional, behavioral and physical signs such as: change of character and mood swings, weight loss, insomnia, physical fatigue, verbal expression of their intention about suicide, isolation or becoming socially withdrawn, loss of interest in the things that were once of interests, and giving their favorite items to others (Suicide Prevention Services, 25th May, 2010).

Stress and Teachers in Hong Kong

A recent research study on Hong Kong teachers' stress, conducted by the Hong Kong Primary Education Research Association and Education

Convergence, revealed that primary and secondary school teachers suffered from large amount of work-related pressures. They are mainly from student misbehavior, expectations of teachers' professional standard, school administration and management, time management and workload issues, and teachers' self-efficacy in student support and career development (Hong Kong Primary Education Research Association and Education Convergence, p.35). Besides, the uncertainties of education reform, class reduction and school killing policies also brought huge pressure to teachers. Another survey conducted by the Hong Kong Professional Teacher Union also disclosed that over 50% of teachers suffered from tension, muscle pain and physical fatigue, which are signs and symptoms of stress arousal phase (Hong Kong Professional Teachers' Union, 2005, p.6). The longer the teaching experience, the greater the stress faced by the teachers. About 64% of teachers suffered pressure from non-school hour workload for more than 31 hours per week. Most of the teachers suffered from exhaustion but few of them take enough rest (Hong Kong Professional Teachers' Union, 2005, p.14). According to the survey, teachers chose not to take sick leave even if they suffered from high pressure, because they did not want to interfere with the teaching schedule. They had a high workload of administrative work to do, and they felt pressure from the principal. After the sick leave, they needed to cope with extra workload; this again created another huge pressure for teachers (Hong Kong Professional Teachers' Union, 2005, p.11). Research also reveals that teachers feel greater pressure in November, May and June. There have been numerous teacher suicide cases related to their work-related pressure for the past decade.

According to a study done by the Hong Kong Mood Disorder Centre, there is a relationship between work-related stress and emotional illness (Hong Kong Mood Disorders Centre, 25th May, 2010). There were between 19.7% and 13.8% of teachers having depression and generalized anxiety disorder. 8.3% of teachers have both depression and generalized anxiety disorder. (Hong Kong Mood Disorders Centre, 25th May, 2010), and they are more likely to commit suicide than others.

CONTENT

Cases Illustration

Ms. Yung, a female teacher aged 37, married. She was a form one mistress, responsible for Girl Guide, and was teaching liberal studies and home economics. A loud noise was suddenly heard in the school campaign, and Ms. Yung was found lying unconscious on the school cover playground. She leaped to her death in front of about 20 students. She fell from the floor corridor of the school. About 20 students who saw what happened were emotionally distraught and were being counseled by clinical psychologists. The school principal said the school had not heard of the teacher needing assistance or having issues relating to work pressure. The Education Bureau said it was saddened by her death (South China Morning Post, 27 April, 2010.).

Crisis Management Team

The crisis management team (CMT) consists of the principal, vice principal, a master teacher of the disciplinary team, a master teacher of guidance and counseling team, and a school social worker, as shown in Table 1. The crisis management team (CMT) in a school work together to prevent and control the crisis when teacher suicide happens in school in order to minimize the impact of the crisis (Devlin, 2007, p.2)

Crisis Management Plan

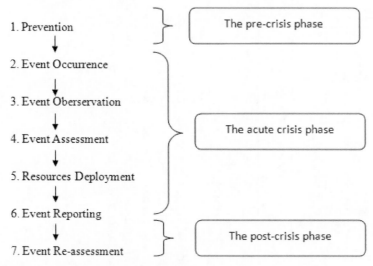

Modified from Dantas, & Seville, and Mitchell and Everly.

Figure 1. Crisis Management plan.

Table 1. A Crisis Management Team (CMT) is set up in school

Team member	Staff	Duties
Director	Principal	Calling the crisis management team and initiating the phone chain if necessary.
Vice-chairperson	Vice principal	Communicating the official version of the event that will be communicated to staff, students, parents and press.
Member	Master teacher of disciplinary team	Ensuring the equipment is available. Calling the police as necessary.
Member	Master teacher of guidance and counseling team, and the school social worker	Counseling of students, teachers and parents during any crisis situation.

The principal is the director. He or she is responsible for calling the crisis management team and for initiating the phone chain if necessary. The vice principal will communicate the official version of the event that will be communicated to staff, students, parents and press. The master teacher of the disciplinary team is responsible for calling the police as necessary. The master teacher of the guidance and counseling team and school social worker is responsible for the counseling of students, teachers and parents during any crisis situation.

It is responsible for leading the school in emergency procedures, looking for ways in pre-impact, impact, post-impact and recovery phases in cases of the event of teacher suicide incident. It ensures the equipment is available in the emergency phase, and contacts students, teachers, parents and press appropriately. If one of the team members is unavailable, directors have to assign another team member to replace the duty (Ling To Catholic Primary School, 25th May, 2010).

The Pre-Crisis phase

1. Prevention

Firstly, colleagues in school can express concern and offer teachers support. They can be aware of the common cognitive, physical, emotional and behavioral signs and symptoms of excessive stress of teachers: cognitive signs such as confusion in thinking and difficulty in making decisions; physical signs such as excessive sweating, dizzy spells and rapid breathing; emotional signs such as anger, grief, depression and hopeless;and behavioral signs, such as changing ordinary behavior patterns, withdrawal from others and prolonged silences (Mitchell, Everly, 1989, p.52). Referrals to the school social worker or education psychologists is needed if teachers are reaching the exhaustion phase in which the above symptoms keep appearing. Also, psychologists can inform the school to cut down the unbearable workload of the teachers for a short period of time or letg them have sick leave if possible.

Secondly, schools can provide stress management workshops for teachers with high stress, especially in November, May and June, which are the months teachers suffered from the highest pressure. The workshops aim at teaching teachers appropriate stress management techniques: 1. Techniques to avoid or reduce exposure to stressors, such as problem solving skills, time management, nutritional techniques and skills in avoiding known stressors. 2. Techniques to reappraise or reinterpret stressors, such as cognitive reframing, psychotherapy. 3. Techniques to reduce stress arousal, such as proper sleep patterns, relaxation response training and prescription anxiolytic medications. 4. Techniques to ventilate the stress arousal, such as physical exercise and catharsis (Mitchell, Everly, 1989, p.41).

The Acute Crisis Phase

2. Event Occurrence

School colleagues should be sensitive when the person speaks of clear-cut self-destructive plans. They should stay with a suicidal person if there seems to be immediate danger, and call on the crisis management team and whoever is needed. They should also not try to handle everything alone.

Immediate action should be taken when the teacher is attempting suicide. The director of crisis management team should be clear about what is happening. He or she has to identify the needs of the incident and direct the team members immediately. The master teacher of the guidance and counseling team and school social worker can show concern and care for the victim in order to prevent the incident; the victim should not be left alone. The master teacher of the disciplinary team has to contact the emergency helpline immediately, keep all kinds of weapons away from the victim, and make sure the environment is out of danger and all students are kept away from the place (HKJC Centre for Suicide Research and Prevention, view on 25th May, 2010).

3. Event Observation

The response plan should be clearly specified and understood by the crisis management team. The team members should prepare themselves well before they need to manage the incident and respond to other staff, students, parents and the community. Contact the emergency helpline immediately. Make sure the environment is out of danger and all students are kept away from the place. Inform the Education Bureau to seek assistance. (HKJC Centre for Suicide Research and Prevention, 25th May, 2010). The school social worker and education psychologists have to provide immediate counsel to students and teachers who have witnessed the incident and are emotionally distraught. The director has to make special arrangements for the school day, and prepare the announcement made to the whole school and the media (HKJC Centre for Suicide Research and Prevention, 25th May, 2010).

4. Event Assessment

The crisis management team has to hold a meetingand compare the situation before and after the incident, evaluate the actions that have been taken, and report on the different needs of victim's family, school, teachers, students and parents. Moreover, the team members have to design a plan for effective resource allocation and effective follow-up. Following implementation of the plan, it should be reviewed and evaluated, and long term issues emerging from the suicide should be addressed (HKJC Centre for Suicide Research and Prevention, 25th May, 2010).

5. Resources Deployment

Both short term and long term resource allocation plans need to be considered. The needs of all members of the school community need to be carefully considered, and after evaluation, the appropriate actions needed to be taken (HKJC Centre for Suicide Research and Prevention, 25th May, 2010), such as immediate and follow-up counseling for those who suffered, and the organization of workshops for teachers and students to promote healthy life messages after the incident.

6. Event Reporting

There needs to be a distribution of a written and verbal statement, to inform students, teachers, parents and media about what has happened, that shows grief and respect to the teacher who has commit suicide. The message should be conveyed to students that suicide is not a good choice. It is much more meaningful for them to seek out solutions other than suicide. If they come across any difficulties, teachers and parents wish to help them. The message should be conveyed to teachers that schools will always provide individual assistance if teachers are facing huge pressure. Also, the school should equip staff with an appropriate response after the traumatic event and encourage teachers to express concern to each other and to notice whether colleagues show stress-related symptoms.

7. Event Re-assessment

The crisis management team has to hold regular meetings, evaluate the existing crisis management plan for handling teacher suicide, identify the potential risk factors that will cause teacher suicide incidents, plan for effective resource allocation, evaluate the existing school mechanism, and assign reasonable working hours and workload to teachers. Is should also provide enough channels for teachers to express their voice and provide long-term individual assistance for teachers who are at high risk.

IMPLICATIONS FOR CRISIS PREVENTION

A proverb states, "Prevention is better than cure." It is suggested that more emphasis is needed to be put on the pre-crisis phase of this plan to prevent tragedy from happening. It is believed that lively opportunity is everywhere. People who are suicidal, in despair, or who have emotional distress, may be affected by the true heart of someone, and they may share the belief of someone that there is always someone concerned about others. Never neglect to contact the voice of teachers, to understand the needs of teachers and to empathize with the emotions of teachers. Always listen, care and be sensitive to them to prevent the crisis (The Samaritan Befrienders Hong Kong, 25th May, 2010).

It is also important for schools to promote a healthy, harmonious and caring working environment for teachers, who spend at least 9 hours per working day in it. It is suggested that schools can provide adequate resources and support to teachers when they are coping with pressure. For example, schools can provide more recreational activities, hold mind and soul reconstruction classes or to offer days of sick leave for those who need it.

DISCUSSION

The crisis management plan for handling teacher suicide is important for schools. It is believed that if schools have given out enough guidelines to teachers on how to prevent and handle the situation of teacher suicide, teachers will be more calm and confident in preventing the crisis, managing the crisis and following up on the crisis instead of everything being beyond their control.

It is suggested that the plan should be issued by the Education Bureau (EDB) to all primary and secondary schools, followed by a briefing session for all principals on how to implement the plan in schools. Every school is different and unique in its makeup of staff, its students, its parents and surrounding community. It is also suggested that the school crisis management team (CMT) should make necessary adaptations to suit the school's needs, provide a clear framework and useful guiding principles to all teachers based on this plan and their school's own features. The framework and guidelines should be posted on the staff room notice board and be printed in the teacher's handbook, which help school teachers familiarize themselves with its operational detailsso they are well prepared when a crisis does occur (St Mary Canossian College, view on 25th May, 2010).

However, there is still a question as to whether this crisis management plan can be comprehensively promoted in schools. It is a fact that Hong Kong teachers are burdened with a huge workload including preparing teaching materials, organizing extra-curricular activities, counseling students etc. There is little time for teachers rest in school, let alone join the recreational activities and classes as suggested above. A lot of teachers are not willing to take sick leave even they are under great work-related pressure, because they feel pressure from the principal. Most bosses have a bad impression of someone having depression or mental illness, and they may not be willing to hire them long term. In order to keep their job, most teachers do not tell others even if they are aware of their emotional symptoms. This means the high risk groups are lacking support and they are putting themselves in danger.

CONCLUSION

No one knows when and where crisis will happen. So, hope for the best and prepare for the worst, aiming at satisfying the needs of all stakeholders involved and redressing the equilibrium of schools routines once they are disrupted.

Education is not only teaching and learning, but life affecting life. It is important for teachers to nurture students to be the masters of our future society. But how can students grow healthy if their teachers have serious physical exhaustion problems, negative emotions and even emotional illnesses? Also, there must be a long period of time for the healing of students' minds and souls if they experience the crisis of teacher suicide. We should face this problem directly. It is never too late to implement this crisis management plan for handling teacher suicide in schools.

ABOUT THE AUTHOR

Lee Yi is a home economics teacher in a secondary school. She has been working in the school for 3 years. She has completed her Degree of Education in the Hong Kong Institute of Education, majoring in home economics. She is furthering her master's studies related to health education at the Chinese

University of Hong Kong. The email address of the author is ceci0215@yahoo.com.hk.

REFERENCES

Chan, S. F., and Chan, Z. C. Y. (2009). Food safety crisis management plan in Hong Kong. *Journal of Food Safety, 29*, 394-413.

Crisis Management, Education Bureau (EDB). View from http://ww w.edb.gov.hk/index.aspx?nodeID=2316&langno=1 on 25th May, 2010.

Coroner's Court services and facilities. View from http://www.judiciary .gov.hk/en/crt_services/pphlt/html/cor.htm on 25th May, 2010.

Dantas, A., Seville, E. (2006). Organisational issues in implementing an information sharing framework: Lessons from the Matata flooding events in New Zealand. *Journal of Contingencies and Crisis Management, 14*(1), 38-52.

Hong Kong Mood Disorders Centre, the Chinese University of Hong Kong. Viewfrom http://www.hmdc.med.cuhk.edu.hk/main.html on 25th May, 2010.

HKJC Centre for Suicide Research and Prevention. View from *http:// csrp.hku.hk/WEB/eng/index.asp* on 25th May, 2010. The University of Hong Kong.

Hong Kong Primary Education Research Association and Education Convergence. *Education Research Report Series (2) A Research Study on Hong Kong Teachers' Stress: Preliminary Analysis*, 12. 2006

Hong Kong Professional Teachers' Union (2005). *A Research Study on Hong Kong Teachers' Stress*.

Hui, K. L., & Chan, Z. C. Y. (2009). Crisis Management Plan in an Episode of Infection of H5N1 in Poultry Workers. In Zenobia C. Y. Chan ed. *Health issues in Chinese contexts Vol 2*. New York: Nova Science Publishers, Inc.

Mitchell Jeffrey T, Everly, Jr. (1989). *Critical Incident Stress Management (CISM): Basic Group Crisis Intervention*. International Critical Incident Stress Foundation.

Ling To Catholic Primary School. View from http://www.lingto.edu.hk on 25th May, 2010.

Ip, Q. T. Y., & Chan, Z. C. Y. (2009). Crisis management plan for health and beauty care accidents. In Zenobia C. Y. Chan ed. *Health issues in Chinese contexts Vol 3*. New York: Nova Science Publishers, Inc.

Lee, S. Y., & Chan, Z. C. Y. (2009). Applying Crisis Management Plans to Public Transportation Accidents. In Zenobia C. Y. Chan ed. *Health issues in Chinese Contexts Vol 2*. New York: Nova Science Publishers, Inc.

Shang, W., & Hooker, N. H. (2005). Improving recall crisis management: should retailer information be disclosed? *Journal of Public Affairs, 5*, 329-341.

Suicide Prevention Services, View from: http://www.sps.org.hk/index_en.php?&cid=2&id=11#title1 on 25th May, 2010.

South China Morning Post, *Teacher leaps to death in front of student*, View on 27 April, 2010.

St Mary Canossian College. View from http://www.smcc-canossian.org/intranet/crisis/crisise.pdf on 25th May, 2010.

The Hong Kong Jockey Club Centre for Suicide Research and Prevention, The University of Hong Kong, suicide rate in Hong Kong from 1999-2007. View from http://www.sps.org.hk/index_en.php?cid=2&id=11&pid=3 on 25th May, 2010.

The Samaritan Befrienders Hong Kong. View from http:// www.sbhk .org .hk/en_gen_intro03.htm#grow on 25th May, 2010.

In: Crisis Management in Chinese Contexts   ISBN: 978-1-61761-609-9
Editor: Zenbobia C. Y. Chan   © 2011 Nova Science Publishers, Inc.

Chapter 10

PREPAREDNESS IN LARGE SCALE DRUG RECALL

Y. W. So[1] and Zenobia C. Y. Chan

School of Nursing, The Hong Kong Polytechnic University

SUMMARY

This chapter aims to illustrate the importance of public relations skills during a drug recall crisis. The proper crisis management in a drug recall is necessary for the manufacturer to reduce the impact on its reputation. It is also important for the government to retain the public's confidence in their ability to protect citizens' health. In a large scale drug recall, which involves a vast number of patients making it difficult to contact those affected patients, the government should coordinate the whole drug recall procedure so that the chaos can be minimized and general public will find the government to be a caring organization looking after Hong Kong's citizens.

---

[1] Email: ewan_so@hotmail.com

INTRODUCTION

Drug Recall System

Since late 1990s, the Department of Health, the regulatory body of pharmaceutical issues in Hong Kong, has adopted the Good Manufacturing Practices (GMP) standard promulgated by the World Health Organization (WHO). Within the GMP there is a recall handling guideline for pharmaceutical manufacturers, wholesalers and retailers to follow. The Department of Health may order the drug company to uphold a voluntary recall for the sake of general public's health. Since there should be a transaction record held by the suppliers including manufacturers, wholesalers and retailers, the drug recall procedure would then be easily carried out. During the recall system, the supplier may inform the customers (wholesalers, importers and retailers) to withhold the concerned batches of medicines and also to deal with the refund or exchange for another batch of products. For instance, if the drug manufacturer finds the printing of the drug label is not correct, he should report it to Department of Health immediately, describe the incident and the action decided. The Department of Health will instruct the manufacturer to carry out the recall procedure.

Pharmaceutical Incidents in Hong Kong

A contaminated drug incident which happened in Hong Kong in March 2009, resulted in several people dying. The contaminated drug was allopurinal, which is used to treat hyperuricemia and prevent attacks of gout. Laboratory testing showed the drug was contaminated by fungus. In those patients suffering from immunosuppressive disease, the ingestion of the contaminated drugs caused a severe fungal infection. A macro drug recall of the pharmaceutical product was announced by the Department of Health, Hong Kong Special Administrative Region (HKSAR). Hospital Authority, an organization that manages the public hospitals and clinics, soon arranged a grand recall action for the public patients to exchange other brands containing the same medicinal ingredient to the affected patients. At that time, Hospital Authority placed many orders with this manufacturer to supply several different drugs to all public hospitals and clinics. The Department of Health ordered this manufacturer to stop all the production within this plant. With its closure of the plant, all the production lines needed to halt. Since the manufacturer is the sole company to supply this high volume product to the public patients, this presented a great challenge to Hospital Authority. Those assigned to procurement withinHospital Authority needed to search for different sources and different suppliers to provide the adequate amount of drugs to the public patients among the public hospitals and clinics in a very short time. The new supply of allopurinal was not enough for the total replacement of the contaminated batches. Therefore, an urgent recall was announced through mass media. Patients who were receiving allopurinal had bring their stocks back to hospital pharmacies in order to exchange them for another brand, but the quantity was adequate only for 4 weeks. Patients were required to come back 4 weeks later. This extra recall action brought extra workload to the hospital pharmacies. Apart from that, patients who collected the medicines from the hospital would ask the pharmacy staff whether their medication was safe to use. The pharmaceutical incident definitely lowered the reputation of the public healthcare system and also the confidence in the local pharmaceutical manufacturer.

Even though the consultation document was finished and 75 recommendations were made on December 2009, several pharmaceutical incidents still happened in 2010. In March 2010, the Department of Health warned that Po Chai pills, a proprietary Chinese medicine, was contaminated with the unlisted western medicines, sibutramine and phenolphthalein. This Po Chai pill was one of the famous proprietary Chinese medicines for gastrointestinal upset. The Department of Health asked the manufacturer to recall those affected products and provided a hotline for the general public. The next day people found difficulty in returning the faulty products; many people complained the government did not collaborate well on the recall procedure. On May 7, 2010 the Department of Health announced a total recall of a local pharmaceutical manufacturer, Quality Pharmaceutical Laboratory. The qualities of its several products were found as not achieving the standard. The government provided a hotline, but, at the same time, it did not announce the recall procedure. Those patients who were taking the affected medicine could not realize how to react. Patients did not know whether their drugs were made by this manufacturer. People expect the government to deliver the affected batch of concerned products together with a comprehensive recall logistic.

SEVERITY OF DRUG RECALL

It is important to define the severity of the pharmaceutical incidents. How the different drug recall procedures would be carried out depends on the level of the severity.

	Small Scale Drug Recall	Large Scale Drug Recall
Involved Institution	Only one	Two or more
Contact of affected clients	Easily contacted	Difficult to contact

If the pharmaceutical incident happens within an institution, for instance, some expired cough mixture was dispensed by a public clinic, the affected patients can be easily traced, and the institution may organize the recall itself. However, if during the production process the quality of the products were found to be below the standard and were sold to a vast number of patients, mass media would be a good channel to announce the information and the arrangement for that kind of recall – large scale drug recall.

PUBLIC RELATIONS IN CRISIS MANAGEMENT

Crisis Management

Crisis management aims to confine or minimize any damage to the organization's reputation or image (Devlin, 2007). Julia Gabis emphasized that good crisis management should not only minimize the danger affecting the organization but also maximize every possible opportunity. A crisis can also be a situation where, in the eyes of the media or general public, the organization did not react in the appropriate manner. In crisis management, the threat is the potential damage of an organization, its stakeholders, and an industry. A crisis can create three related threats: (1) public safety, (2) financial loss, and (3) reputation loss. These three threats are interrelated. Injuries or deaths will result in financial and reputation losses, while reputations have a financial impact on organizations.

An excellent crisis management case is the Tylenol Poisoning Incident of 1982, where the chief executive officer (CEO) reacted fast and cooperated well with mass media. The practice of public relations can play a critical role in a crisis situation. There are three objectives of public relations in crisis management:

1) Prevent, if possible
2) Modify negative effects
3) Provide a platform for the organization's future

A pharmaceutical incident is unpredicted; it is a kind of crisis that happens wth the manufacturer. The reputation and the organizational image will drop sharply. The leader of the company should never try to mask the incident, and should tell the truth. The leader should also not procrastinate the necessary action, or the crisis will become worse. One should react fast and appropriately to the incidents occuring at the early stage.

Usually, people will think a drug recall is the matter of the pharmaceutical manufacturer; the problems should be solved by that drug company. But drug recalls are a matter of public health, no matter if it is on a small or big scale. If the problems are not handled properly, patients' health may deteriorate. There may be severe consequences if the patients cannot receive the proper pharmacotherapy. There is also a political consideration: when the manufacturer does not react well to the drug recall action, the general public will blame the government. Citizens will query about why the government did not monitor the industry more closely and why the government did not coordinate the recall procedure properly. In a large scale drug recall, it is important for the government to coordinate well between the public hospitals, public clinics, private hospital, private clinics and retail pharmacies. The communication between the Department of Health and these organizations should be effective so that the whole recall procedure can be understood by all parties. Mass media, including electronic media (they are 24 hours broadcasting), newspapers and radio should be acknowledged at all times. If any wrong message is being delivered, a chaotic situation may happen. After crisis is settled, a review should be carried out and find ways to improve the whole procedure.

Tylenol Poisoning

The practice of public relations is valuable to a company. Customers are willing to pay more for a manufacturer they trust. Building up the reputation and the positive image of a company is a great task for the manager. Also, such merit cannot be easily established in a short time. However, the confidence or the trust of the customers will fall immediately if a product recall occurs. The profit will drop substantially and if the manager does not react to the incident properly, and on time, the crisis will become enlarged. A famous pharmaceutical product recall happened in September 1982 in the Chicago area of the United States. The pain killer Tylenol, manufactured by Johnson & Johnson's (J&J), was found to be contaminated with cyanide, a very toxic chemical. Seven people died from ingesting the poisonous substance. After the investigation, the it was found that the contamination did not occur as a result of the manufacturing process.. A week later, the CEO James E. Burke announced a nationwide recall of Tylenol products. In addition to organizing the drug recall, J&J established relations with the Chicago Police, the FBI, and the Food and Drug Administration to investigate and search for the person who laced the Tylenol and to help prevent further tampering. This incident was reported by the mass media positively at that time because J&J announced that public safety was far more important than the company's profit. The skillful public relations practiced by the company, therefore, plays an important role in helping the organization recover from crisis. The Tylenol fast acting recall maintained the company's reputation and the business was able to bounce back.

Toyota Recall

Several incidents were reported in which the vehicles made by Toyota were found to have some faults, including the vehicle accelerating automatically. The manufacturer responded to the incidents slowly; the management was led by the media all along. Then, Toyota employed multimedia resources to address its customers using a consistent tone and message. The tone was serious and the messages expressed apology, working to rectify the problems and to restore customer confidence.

The company's web site has a link right on the front page. The link takes visitors to well-organized information pages with lists of recalled vehicles, problems, and solutions. To their credit, the web site has been kept up-to-date with current information.

The most effective crisis management takes place before the problem escalates out of control during the "incubation" phase. Some of the serious potential crises have been identified and addressed before they ever got out of control: this is crisis management at its best. This requires an organizational culture that is vigilant about potential crises, has open lines of communication betweem staff and management, and is willing to address unpleasant truths.

The Toyota vehicle recalls demonstrated that the utilization of a website can be an efficient way to deliver a message to the customers, mass media and the general public. Any immediate message can be easily uploaded to the web by the crisis manager. Applying the idea to drug recall, the contaminated or the concerned batches of the products can be listed on the website. The refund scheme and the exchange method can be published and let the public know. The website can be designed as an interactive one. The frontline, including the pharmacies, store, or the clinics, may report to the coordinator and let the top management know more about the real situation. Compared to the traditional method, contact by fax phone, website reporting could be the best way for the communication between the frontlines and the crisis manager.

DISCUSSION

By using the example of Quality Pharmaceutical Laboratory Incident, the Department of Health discovered several products contain less active ingredients than they should. Also, the disintegration time was found to be longer than expected. These cause the drugs to not achieve the desired therapeutic effects in human body. If patients were taking the antibiotics manufactured by this company, not only would the infection not be cured, but even worse than that, drug resistance may then be developed. If a patient was taking psychiatric drugs, their disease may not be well controlled, which may result in a severe consequence. The total product recall of all drugs manufactured by that pharmaceutical company interfered with a vast number of patients in Hong Kong, and these patients were also difficult to contact; it therefore constituted a large scale drug recall crisis.

The Department of Health issued a press release on Friday, May 7, 2010, late at night. This late announcement may have reduced the impact of the incident because the peak influence of electronic media was over (after 10:30p.m. locally). Also, the mass media may have found it difficult to ask some people to make comments on the incident. Therefore, it was a skillful way to announce a challenging issue, late Friday night.

However, the matter of drug recall relates to medical issues; the government should warn the patients or general public as soon as possible or it becomes a moral hazard. The government should protect citizens' health as the first priority and should not bother with its reputation in this case.

CONCLUSION

After several pharmaceutical incidents happened in Hong Kong, whether involving western medicine or proprietary Chinese medicine, the Department of Health still does not react well. The immature crisis management skill is lagging behind the expectation of Hong Kong citizens. The report of the Review Committee on Regulation of Pharmaceutical Products in Hong Kong, published in December 2009, suggested 75 ways to prevent the pharmaceutical incidents from occurring. There are recommendations to strengthen the power of the Department of Health to ask the manufacturer, the wholesaler, and the retailer to cooperate well with the government in order to protect the public's health. The committee also suggested many ways, in addition to the drug recall guidelines established in 2000, to smooth the drug recall procedure in the future. However, the communication between the government and the general public do not meet the expectations of citizens. The government ordered the affected company to carry out a voluntary recall along with providing a hotline for the general public. Citizens, on the other hand, are looking for the actual recall procedures, including the venue(s) collecting the affected drugs, the method of compensation, and the time period. Even with a comprehensive recall guideline and the power to order different parties to cooperate, without sophisticated public relations skills cannot alter the risk into an opportunity to promote government's reputation. We look forward to the improvement of the communication between the government and the general public in Hong Kong.

AUTHOR'S BACKGROUND

Yiu-Wah So graduated from the University of Nottingham holding a bachelor of pharmacy (with honours) degree, a post-graduate diploma in health care (The Hong Kong Polytechnic University), and is a registered pharmacist (Hong Kong) working at Queen Mary Hospital. The communication email is: ewan_so@hotmail.com.

REFERENCES

(2009). *Report of the Review Committee on Regulation of Pharmaceutical Products in Hong Kong.* Hong Kong: Food and Health Bureau, the Hong Kong Special Administrative Region. http://www.fhb.gov.hk/download /press_and_publications/otherinfo/100105_pharm_review/en_full_report.p df

Altman S. R.(2005). Legal Aspect of Crisis-Management Communication: What to Communicate. *Athletic Therapy Today*, 10(3): 6-10.

Chartier L and Leray C. (2007). *The impact of public relations on organizations' sales – Literature Review.* UQAM Public Relations Chair, 2007.

Devlin E. S. (2007). *Crisis management planning and execution.* Boca Raton: Auerbach Publications.

Shang W. and Hooker N. H. (2005). Improving recall crisis management: should retailer information be disclosed? *Journal of Public Affairs*, 5: 329-341.

Lalonde C. (2004). In Search of Archetypes in Crsis Management. *Journal of Contingencies and Crisis Management*, 12(2): 76-88.

Livet M., Richter J., Ellison L., et al (2005). Emergency Preparedness Academy Adds Public Health to Readiness Equation. *Jounnal of Public Health Management Practice*, November (Suppl):S4-S10.

Luo Y. (2008). A Strategic Analysis of Product Recalls: The Role of Moral Degradation and Organizational Control. *Management and Organization Review*, 4(2): 183-196.

Schouten R., Callahan M. V. and Bryant S. (2004). Community Response to Disaster: The Role of the Workplace. *Harv Rev Psychiatry*, 2004(12): 229-237.

Souiden N. and Pons F. (2009). Product recall crisis management: the impact on manufacturer's image, consumer loyalty and purchase intention. *Journal of Product & Brand Management*, 18(2), 106-114.

Steelfisher G. et al (2010). Public Perceptions of Food Recalls and Production Safety: Two Surveys of the American Public. *Journal of Food Safety*, 2010.

Torbeck L., Friedman R., Smedley M. (2009). An Overview of the CDER Drug Recall Root Cause Research Project. *Pharmaceutical Technology*, 33(8): 42-45.

In: Crisis Management in Chinese Contexts   ISBN: 978-1-61761-609-9
Editor: Zenbobia C. Y. Chan   © 2011 Nova Science Publishers, Inc.

Chapter 11

CRISIS MANAGEMENT PLAN OF HUMAN SWINE INFLUENZA IN HOSPITAL SETTING

N. Y. Lam[1] and Zenobia C. Y. Chan

School of Nursing, The Hong Kong Polytechnic University

SUMMARY

Crisis management teams need to make decisions; they also need to increase the awareness of the project through regular meetings. The chairman of the crisis management team has power to alert and mobilize the involved parties. The crisis management team needs to learn from history. Training and drills need to be provided to the appropriate peple; all leaders should be well prepared and know what they should do when a crisis happens. This chapter suggests a well-designed crisis management plan for human swine influenza in a hospital setting to prevent the situation from becoming worse when a disaster happens.

BACKGROUND

Every year there is a different kind of influenza outbreak. In 2009, there was a new influenza - human swine influenza (H1N1) - out break in North

---

[1] Email: cherrysky1012@yahoo.com.hk

America which then spread around the world. It will increase demands for health care service.

There are two health care systems in Hong Kong: the public and private sectors. Most people use public health care system (Wong, Y. Y., & Chan, Z. C. Y. 2009). There are 41 public hospitals, 28 specialist outpatient clinics, and 74 general outpatient clinics under Hospital Authority. It is formed by seven hospital clusters, according to location. Although there are many hospitals, the occupancy rate is very high and manpower is quite tight. If a crisis happens, Hospital Authority not only needs to remain in service but also needs to spare manpower, money, facilities, etc. to manage the crisis. It is not an easy thing to make a decision in a short time, So Hospital Authority needs a crisis management plan to solve the problem, and try to minimize the harmful effecs on Hospital Authority (Devlin, E. S. 2007).

H1N1 is a virus; it is transmitted from person to person through contact and droplets. H1N1 is type A influenza. Signs and symptoms include high fever, sore throat, cough, running nose, headache, muscle pain, joint pain, generalized malaise. The incubation period is around 48 hours. Patients can heal without medication in a week, but it can also cause death (World Health Organization 2010).

Influenza can affect all age groups. However, children younger than two years old, elderly people older than 65 years old, and patients suffering from chronic diseases have a higher risk of complications (World Health Organization 2010).

From May 1, 2009 to May 29, 2010, there were a total of 282 severe human swine influenza cases: 171 cases were male, 111 cases were female; their ages were between 30 to 95 years old. There was a total of 80 fatal cases: 56 cases were male and 24 cases were female; their ages were between one and 95 years old (Department of Health 2010).

As of May 28, 2010 there were over 214 countries reporting cases of pandemic influenza H1N1; 18,114 cases died (World Health Organization 2010). Many human swine influenza patients need services from hospitals. So, crisis management plans for human swine influenza in a hospital setting is very important.

For respiratory hygiene or cough etiquette in healthcare settings, the Department of Health suggests that people should let health care providers know about their symptoms of respiratory infection when they go to a hospital, whether the are there to see doctor, have treatment, or visit a patient. If people have respiratory symptoms, they should wear surgical masks. When coughing or sneezing, they should cover their nose and mouth with tissue paper then dispose of it in a rubbish bin with a lid. They should wash hands or perform hand rub after contaminated by respiratory secretion. People with respiratory symptoms should be separatedfrom others by at least one meter (World Health Organization 2007).

OBJECTIVE

This article identifies the preventive phase of crisis management for human swine influenza in hospital setting. In preventive phase, I will identify different situations in the acute stage, then divide different jobs among different parties, set up standard practices, pass along authoritative decisions, establish communication systems and provide training to involved parties to prevent and slow down the spread of human swine influenza in the hospital. It can reduce morbidity and mortality when the crisis happens (Schouten, R., Callahan, M. V., & Bryant, S). Proper preparation can change negative results into positive results (Lalonde, C. 2004).

RATIONALES

This project focuses on the pre-crisis stage (known as the precursor stage) which is prior to the critical situation and Hospital Authority's action in the crisis. In this stage, Hospital Authority needs to analyze all information to estimate the potential of crisis. To identify pre-crisis alarm and prevent negative impact on the Hospital Authority, we need a crisis management plan. If we do not handle pre-crisis well, it will move to the acute crisis stage and the situation will get worse.

There are three levels of preparedness: low, medium and high. As the situation becomes more important, the level of preparedness will increase (McConnell, A., & Drennan, L. 2006). I suggest that the crisis management team should have regular meetings to monitor the situation and prevent underestimation, overestimation and overlooking of the warning signals (Devlin, E. S. 2007).

REVIEW OF LITERATURE

The chance of crisis happening is low. When crisis happens, it will surprise Hospital Authority since they do not understand the process of crisis. It is difficult to make decisions (Runyan, R. C. 2006).

Crisis is unexpected, has high level of uncertainly and is severe, so, when facing crisis, decisions should be made rapidly. Research indicates needs assessment, and recognizing and obtaining resources, allows for better performance and more effective crisis response. It can save more lives (Galambos, C. M. 2005).

In crisis management, there are seven principles. This program uses these principles as a framework:

1) Before making decisions, gain opinions from multiple parties.
2) Closely monitor the implementation of the program.
3) Be effective.
4) Set the aims.
5) Be flexible.
6) Know the nature of and potential for risk.
7) Keep good communication. (Devlin, E. S. 2007)

INFECTION IN HUMANS

It is caused by the novel influenza (H1N1) virus. In April 2009, it was discovered in North America, and spread around the world. (World Health Organization 2010).

MODE OF TRANSMISSION

It spreads from person to person; the patient spills out the virus when coughing and sneezing. After touching the mouth, nose, and eyes of patient directly, or touching a soiled object, there can also be infection. There is no evidence to show that human swine influenza can be transmitted through eating processed pork or other food products derived from pigs. H1N1 can be killed if the temperature is higher than 70°C (160°F). H1N1 can live two hours or longer on an object. (World Health Organization 2010).

SIGN AND SYMPTOMS

The symptoms of human swine influenza are similar to human seasonal influenza. They include high fever, sore throat, cough, runny nose, headache, muscle pain, joint pain, and generalized malaise. Some patients will have nausea, vomiting and diarrhea (World Health Organization 2010).

In severe cases, it may cause death. If a pregnant woman is infected, is may affect the fetus (World Health Organization 2010).

VACCINATION

In December 2009, a vaccination scheme for human swine influenza was started. Five target groups can get free vaccinations at public, and some private, clinics that joined the subsidy scheme. The target groups include: health care providers; chronic illness patients and pregnant women; children from 6 months to 6 years old; elderly people who are 65 years old or older; and pig farmers and pig-slaughtering industry personnel (World Health Organization 2010).

However, there are only 191,068 people who have had the human swine influenza vaccination since the vaccination program started. After vaccination, there were 8 cases of spontaneous abortion, one case died, and 11 cases have different health problems (World Health Organization 2010).

Low vaccination rate will effect long term care in influenza outbreak; it will also increase the infection rate (Hrehocik, M. 2008).

TREATMENT

In the early stage of illness, patient can use Oseltamivir (known as Tamiflu) or Zanamivir (known as Relenza) with a doctor's prescription, as human swine influenza virus is sensitive to these two kinds of antiviral medication. However, pregnant women cannot use these two medications since there is no clinical study to prove it is safe to pregnant woman and the fetus.

Side effects of Oseltamivir are bronchitis, dizziness, nausea, vomiting and diarrhea. Side effects of gastrointestinal upset can be reduced if the medication is taken after food.

SOCIAL IMPACT OF HUMAN SWINE INFLUENZA

The expert group already states that the human swine influenza vaccine is safe, but the vaccination rate is quite low. The Hong Kong government used seven billion to buy three million human swine influenza vaccines, but less than 10% of the vaccines were used. The reaction of citizens is difficult to predict. If Hong Kong did not have enough vaccines, they would worry. It may affect the stability of the society.

FLOW OF CRISIS MANAGEMENT ACTION PLAN

Review Human Swine Influenza plan > Perform needs assessment for involved parties > Assess power of Hospital Authority> Fix the scope of the plan > Identify the aim > Develop schedule > Send exercise directive > Form design team > Establish evaluation team > Compose objective > Make Narrative > Record major circumstances in detail> Confirm expected action > List messages> Finalize exercise enhancements > Develop evaluation plan (World Health Organization 2009).

INSTANT ASSESSMENT

1) Assess the knowledge of and response to human swine influenza. Give some tests about human swine influenza to all health care providers in hospital to check what they know and what should or should not be done.
2) Assess the response of the crisis management team. They should have regular meetings and make sure all members of the management team know what they should do if human swine influenza spreads in the hospital.
3) Assess internal-organization and external-organization coordination. Have regular drills to test their organization techniques.
4) Assess each hazard of human swine influenza. Observe the trend of human swine influenza in the world.
5) Assess the training of involved parties. Make sure all involved parties have proper training.

6) Assess drills and exercises. Make sure there are enough proper drills and exercises.
7) Assess the ongoing process. All involved parties should monitor the progress of the crisis management team (Perry and Lindell 2003).

SETTING UP A CRISIS MANAGEMENT TEAM

In Hospital Authority, there is a chief executive, regional advisory committees, hospital governing committees, the hospital chief executive, and the following deputy directors: business support services, corporate affairs, finance, financial development, hospital planning and development, management/ human sources, information systems, management, operations, deputy operations and service development, and public affairs.

The progressive program will involve different departments; their coordination with each other are very important for the emergency management (World Health Organization 2009). As the situation is very complicated, if they want to have win-win solution, they should have more communication to understand all parties' situations and difficulties. After the whole picture is known, the crisis management team will be more constructive and creative (Weitzman, E. A., & Kew, D. 2002).

The crisis management team should monitor the trend of human swine influenza. It is important that members have a high level of self awareness (monitoring their emotional problems) and team awareness (be concern with members' needs and help them) (Mclennan, J., Holgate, A. M., Omodei, M. M., & Wearing, A. J. 2006). If the members cannot handle their stress and emotional problems, it will affect their performance. Crisis management team members need to initiate and implement the crisis management plan (Gourlay, C. 2004).

STRATEGIES

Before a human swine influenza outbreak:

1) Set up a human swine influenza crisis management team. The chief executive of Hospital Authority will act as the chairman. He decides his team members, which members to deputize, assigns appropriate jobs to the right peopleand sets the frequency of the meetings. All

involved parties will be informed of the resolutions made by the crisis management team.

2) Set up guidelines about training, treatment, and prevention.

3) The infection disease control training center and human resources department ensure all staffs have enough infection control training.

4) The finance department needs to make sure there is enough money to buy drugs and protective equipment, for example PPE and masks. It also needs to have a fast-track system to spend money in a crisis and ensure there is special insurance to cover the situation.

5) The human resource department needs to make sure Hospital Authority has enough staff (doctors, nurses and allied health care workers) to serve H1N1 patients. It needs to assign staffs to serve H1N1 patients and have an easy-to-update staff list and contact numbers.

6) The information systems department can analyze the surveillance of human swine influenza and sick leave reports of the staff.

7) The public affairs department can prepare for internal and external communication by preparing and clearing background documents. It also ensures the spokesperson is given enough training and preparation.

8) The hospital planning and development department needs to ensure each hospital has enough isolation facilities, for example, isolation rooms and hand washing facilities.

9) The operations and service development department can set visiting times or disallowto patient visits (The Hong Kong Hospital Authority 2009).

EVALUATION CRITERIA

The effectiveness and efficiency will not only be evaluated by WHO, the government and the crisis management team, but will also be evaluated media, citizens, other countries, etc. Hong Kong will also be compared with other countries. The mortality and mobility rates are the indicators of the success of the human swine influenza crisis management plan.

DISCUSSION

The in-depth assessment, and internal and external communication aspects are significant predictors for the leaders of crisis management team towards implementing a crisis management plan (Tzeng, H. M. 2005). Detecting signals of crisis, researching potential risks, learning from similar crisis experiences, developing training courses, continuing to detect potential crisis and improving the relationship with the media are important (Tzeng, H. M. 2005).

Media plays and important role when crisis happens. The experts, general public, and healthcare professionals will use information from media as a basis to assess their risk (Buus, S., & Olsson, E. K. 2006). Media will request information for headlines, but Hospital Authority needs to protect the privacy of the patient. It may cause conflict. Providing immediate and accurate information to involved parties and the different media can reduce the fear of Hong Kong people (Schouten, R., Callahan, M. V., & Bryant, S).

Different media will have their interpretations; if they blame the everyone understands the whole picture, they will accept the opinion of the media easily. Once they have made up their mind, it is difficult to change. So, the first impression is very important. Spokespeople should be open, honest, accessible, and show empathy and sympathy. He should not answer hypothetical questions. I think people will be easier to accept.

The SARS crisis in 2003 is a good example. The crisis management team was blamed by the media. I think this one of the reason that Hong Kong's people are dissatisfied with the Hong Kong government. No matter what the government does, their thoughts cannot be changed.

CONCLUSION

It is difficult to identify which level of crisis preparedness to use. If high preparedness is used, the cost will increase and will involve many people. However, if low preparednessis used, it may be that the cannot be handled. Crisis management teams will struggle with this. If we can have more frequent meetings and assessments and identify the level of crisis, the the crisis preparedness can be raised or lowered as necessary. I think this will be more cost effective.

Basically, all members need to coordinate with each other, be well prepared and join training and drill programs. They also need to perform planning, implementation and evaluation (Livet, M., Richter, J., Ellison, L., Dease, B., McClure, L., Feigley, C., & richter, D. L. 2005).

Although we have crisis management plans, coordination of rapid and effective response is not easy. Usually before having all the information, crisis management team members have to make decision (Runyan, R. C. 2006). However, if the response to the crisis is appropriate, economic and social impact can be minimized (Dantas, A., & Seville, E. 2006).

This human swine influenza crisis management plan smooths the way for preventing or handling the crisis (Chan, S. F., & Chan, Z. C. Y. 2009). If crisis management team can discuss with the public, it will let all people know the progress. It can lower their degree of anxiety, since this crisis can damage their health and decrease the level of social stability (Chan, Z. C. Y. 2009). When the crisis comes, they will know their responsibilities – for example, wearing surgical masks to protect themselves and others, being aware of their hand hygiene and keeping social distance (Collignon, P. J. & Carnie, J. A. 2006). I hope human swine influenza will not spread in Hong Kong.

AUTHOR'S BACKGROUND

My name is Lam Ngar Yin. I am a registered nurse. I obtained my bachelor of nursing (honors) degree from the University of Hong Kong. I am a second year student at The Chinese University of Hong Kong School of Public Health pursuing my master's of science in health education and promotion. My e-mail address is: cherrysky1012@yahoo.com.hk.

REFERENCES

Buus, S., & Olsson, E. K. (2006). The SARS crisis: was anybody responsible? *Journal of Contingencies and Crisis Management, 14*(2), 71-81.

Chan, S. F., & Chan, Z. C. Y. (2009). Food safety crisis management plan in Hong Kong. *Journal of Food Safety, 29*, 394-413.

Chan, Z. C. Y. (2009). Teaching Crisis Management In Health Care. *Health issues in Chinese contexts Vol 1.* New York: Nova Science Publishers, Inc.

Collignon, P. J. & Carnie, J.A. (2006). Infection control and pandemic influenza. *Medical Journal of Australia, 185*(10). ProQuest Health and Medical Complete

Dantas, A., & Seville, E. (2006). Organisational issues in implementing an information sharing framework: Lessons from the Matata flooding events in New Zealand. *Journal of Contingencies and Crisis Management, 14*(1), 38-52.

Devlin, E. S. (2007). *Crisis management planning and execution.* Boca Raton: Auerbach Publications.

Devlin, E. S. (2007). *Managing through turbulent times.* Boca Raton: Auerbach Publications.

Department of Health. Centre for Health Care Protection.2010, June 3. Swine and Seasonal Flu Monitor. http://www.chp.gov.hk/f iles/pdf/SSFM_3_6_2010.pdf on 6 June 2010.

Galambos, C. M. (2005). Natural disasters: health and mental health considerations. *Health & Social Work, 30*(2), 83-86.

Gourlay, C. (2004). European union procedures and resources for Crisis Management. *International Peacekeeping, 11*(3), 404-421.

Hrehocik, M. (2008). Flu season. *Long-Term Living, 57*(9), Abi/Inform Global

Lalonde, C. (2004). In search of archetypes in crisis management. *Journal of Contingencies and Crisis Management, 12*(2), 76-88.

Livet, M., Richter, J., Ellison, L., Dease, B., McClure, L., Feigley, C., & richter, D. L. (2005). Emergency preparedness academy adds public health to readiness equation. *Journal of Public Health Management Practice*, 4-10.

McConnell, A., & Drennan, L. (2006). Mission impossible? Planning and preparing for crisis. *Journal of Contingencies and Crisis Management, 14*(2), 59-70.

Mclennan, J., Holgate, A. M., Omodei, M. M., & Wearing, A. J. (2006). Decision making effectiveness in wildfire incident management teams. *Journal of Contingencies and Crisis Management, 14*(1), 27-37.

Perry, R.W. and Lindell, M. K. (2003), 'Preparedness for Emergency Response: Guidelines for the Emergency Planning Process', *Disasters,* Volume 27, Number 4, pp. 336-350.

Runyan, R. C. (2006). Small business in the face of crisis: identifying barriers to recovery from a natural disaster. *Journal of Contingencies and Crisis Management, 14*(1), 12-26.

Schouten, R., Callahan, M. V., & Bryant, S. (Community response to disaster: the role of the workplace. *Harvard Review* of *Psychiatry, 12*(4), 229-237.

The Hong Kong Hospital Authority (2009). Checklist of Hospital Authority (HA) Actions for the activation of Emergency Response Levels (E1 and E2) against Human Swine Influenza (HSI). [cited 2010 June 10] Available from: http://www.ha.org.hk/haho/ho/cc/CCC_12Jun2009_new1.pdf

Tzeng, H. M. (2005). Crisis management policies and programs to prevent nursing- related medical disputes in Taiwanese hospitals. *Nursing Economics, 23*(5), 239-247.

Weitzman, E. A., & Kew, D. (2002). Responding to September 11: a conflict resolution scholar/practitioner's perspective. *Analyses of Social Issues and Public Policy*, 109-117.

World Health Organization (2009). *Emergency exercise development.* Western Pacific Region. P. 3.1– p.3.33.

World Health Organization (2010). *Human Swine Influenza.* Retrieved from. http://www.chp.gov.hk/en/view_content/16615.html on 7 June 2010

World Health Organization (2010). *Influenza (Seasonal).* Retrieved from http://www.who.int/mediacentre/factsheets/fs211/en/index.html on 6 June 2010.

World Health Organization (2007). *Isolation precaution.* Retrieved from http://www.chp.gov.hk/files/pdf/ICB_ICG_1.4_Isolation_precautions.pdf on 6 June 2010.

Wong, Y. Y., & Chan, Z. C. Y. (2009). Nursing crisis management: Fire safety in operating theatres. In Zenobia C. Y. Chan ed. *Health issues in Chinese contexts Vol 2*. New York: Nova Science Publishers, Inc.

ABOUT THE EDITOR

Zenobia C. Y. Chan *

Assistant Professor, School of Nursing, The Hong Kong
Polytechnic University

Zenobia Chan is an assistant professor at Hong Kong Polytechnic University School of nursing. She received her bachelor's degree in nursing, and her master's degrees in primary health care and Christian studies, respectively. She obtained a doctoral degree from the Chinese University of Hong. Zenobia loves writing for both its therapeutic and communicative uses. She has written for a wide range of academic journals and has contributed to eight English books (such as Silenced Women, Published by the Nova Science Publishers) and four Chinese books. She has published numerous papers related to nursing, family studies, counseling, mental health, medical education, social work, qualitative research and poetry. In hopes of contributing to Christianity, Zenobia has started her interests in biblical and Christian writings in order to serve as the god servant and deliver the gospels.

* Phone: 852-2766 6426;
Email: hszchan@inet.polyu.edu.hk; zehippo@yahoo.com

INDEX

Q

R

S